Also by DEBRA KAPLAN

For Love and Money: Exploring Sexual
& Financial Betrayal in Relationships

Reflections on the History of the Sex Addiction
Field: A Festschrift (co-editor)

BATTLE
OF THE
TITANS

MASTERING THE FORCES OF SEX, MONEY, AND POWER IN RELATIONSHIPS

DEBRA KAPLAN, MA, MBA, LPC

© 2020 Debra Kaplan

Golden Thread Press

Debra Kaplan
6039 E. Grant Road
Tucson, Arizona, 85712
(520) 203-1943
email: info@debrakaplancounseling.com

www.debrakaplancounseling.com

Cover design by Kat Domet
Book layout by Richard Fenwick

ISBN: 978-0-5787-4602-9

For Jared and Jonah

ADVANCE PRAISE

"Kaplan shines a light on the underbelly that drives the desperate need for money, power, and control—coined Monetary Rage—and its impact on relationships. Recounting her journey with rigorous vulnerability, she skillfully braids together attachment theory, her origin story, and time on Wall Street in a tale that parallels the mythological Greeks jockeying for dominance. *Battle of the Titans* takes us into the inner world of the pathological narcissist with compassion and a healthy dose of reality, while empowering victims toward personal autonomy. An excellent read!"

— **ALEXANDRA KATEHAKIS, Ph.D.**, author of *Sex Addiction as Affect Dysregulation: A Neurobiologically Informed Holistic Treatment*

"Through the clarity of her own life lens, trauma therapist Deb Kaplan, former Wall Street financier, exposes the dark sides of power and control that blindside couples in their relationships. *Battle of the Titans* sheds light on the under- and overevaluation of self, narcissism, sex, money, vulnerabilities, and boundaries. A page-turner of provocative stories, action items, resources, and therapeutic evidence-based support."

— **STAN TATKIN, PsyD.**, author of *We Do: Saying Yes to a Relationship of Depth, True Connection, and Enduring Love*

"Debra Kaplan has given her unique insights into the interaction of sex, money, and power in romantic relationships. Years after writing her first book on the subject, Kaplan has now provided new insights on the roles that psychopathy, narcissism and other personality disorders can play in relationships that have significant power struggles about sex and money. *Battle of the Titans* reflects the author's interesting use of Greek myths and the powerful Greek gods to illustrate the features of the personalities she describes. This very engaging book provides effective tools for couples to establish sexual and financial balance in their relationships. I highly recommend it."

— **JENNIFER P. SCHNEIDER. M.D., Ph.D.**, author of *Back from Betrayal: Recovering from the Trauma of Infidelity and Sex, Lies, & Forgiveness: Couples Speak on Healing from Sex Addiction*

"In *Battle of the Titans*, Kaplan shares fascinating insights on the intersection of power, money, rage, exploitation and narcissistic abuse. Her message of empowerment is critical for anyone struggling with these issues in their relationships. This is a must read for those attempting to break free from financial or sexual exploitation."

— **STEFANIE CARNES, Ph.D.**, author of *Courageous Love: A Couples Guide to Conquering Betrayal*

"Battle of the Titans lays out the path toward more stable and engaged intimacy in 21st century relationships."

— **ROBERT WEISS, Ph.D., LCSW**, Chief Clinical Officer, Seeking Integrity Treatment Programs

"As a financial planner, I often see couples in conflict over money. This book explores and explains the role of money and power in relationships."

— **RICK KAHLER, CFP®, CFT-I™, CeFT®**, co-author of *Conscious Finance* and *The Financial Wisdom of Ebenezer Scrooge*

"*Battle of the Titans* is an engaging narrative connecting the dots between sex, money, and power. Artfully interweaving myth, attachment and personality theories, historical events, case examples, and her own story, Kaplan illustrates how childhood emotional wounds, left unresolved, can form the roots of disrespectful and destructive power imbalances involving sex and money. For those feeling trapped in such relationships, Kaplan guides the reader to balance and well-being by way of self-empowerment. This information provides a new lens for my work as a financial therapist and as a human being."

— **SARAH SWANTNER, CFP®, NCC**

"Debra L. Kaplan eloquently and skillfully sheds light on the dynamics between sex, money, and power in her latest masterpiece, *Battle of the Titans*. She provides excellent tools for couples seeking balance in these areas, and inspires those in abusive relationships to identify exploitive behavior and learn how to protect themselves from the most intimate dangers."

— **CANDICE CHRISTIANSEN, M.Ed., LCMHC, CSAT-S,** Founder of Namasté Center For Healing and The Global Prevention Project®

"Debra takes head-on two of the biggest taboos in our culture—Money and Sex. Leaven that mixture with power and you have a ground breaking book designed to improve any relationship."

— **TED KLONTZ Ph.D.,** Associate Professor of Practice, Financial Psychology Institute, Creighton University, Heider College of Business

CONTENTS

AUTHOR'S NOTE

I have served my clients in diverse therapeutic settings for over two decades—in hospital psychiatric units, first responder crisis and de-escalation emergency services, residential treatment, intensive outpatient settings, workshops, intensives, and individual office settings. Client confidentiality is paramount for me. Accordingly, all individuals and couples presented as illustrative examples within these pages are fictionalized composites. Names and case histories have been radically altered to protect client anonymity. Any similarity to specific people, living or deceased, is entirely coincidental. Stories depicting historical events, however, are real, though accounts here have been condensed for brevity and relevance.

ACKNOWLEDGMENTS

There are many people whose individual and collective contributions helped bring *Battle of the Titans* to life:

Piper J. Daniels was this project's Athena. Her creative coaching and developmental contributions helped me visualize this book. Most importantly, she normalized my writing experience when I became mired in the words or consumed by self-doubt.

I am grateful for Kimberly M. Wetherell and Ami McConnell who joined the editing team with their sleeves rolled up, ready to dig in. I deeply appreciate their editing perspectives that shaped *Battle of the Titans* and pushed it toward the finish line.

In 2017, Dr. Jennifer Schneider invited me to co-edit an anthology on the history of sex addiction, *Reflections on the History of the Sex Addiction Field: A Festschrift.* Jennifer is a gifted writer and editor. Her powerful combination of literary dexterity is over and above her extensive list of accomplishments. She is a physician certified in Internal Medicine, Addiction Medicine and Pain Management, the author of fifteen books and numerous articles in professional journals, and a nationally recognized expert in two addiction-related fields: addictive sexual disorders and the management of chronic pain with opioids. I am grateful that Jennifer so graciously offered to read, reread and edit my manuscript—I am particularly grateful for our friendship.

I want to acknowledge Tracy Barnett. By trade Tracy is a custom homebuilder, but that designation does not do her craft justice. Tracy constructs residential masterpieces from the ground up. When she turns over the keys, the owner receives an awe-inspiring home with a rich soul—built with love and a fastidious attention to detail. Tracy read versions of the manuscript the way she builds homes; with passion and attention to detail—thank you, Tracy!

A big thank you to Richard Fenwick for his expertise in formatting and interior design of the book; and to Kat Domet and Leslie Howard for their graphic design and voice talent, respectively.

Thank you to the many individuals and couples who have trusted me with their emotional lives. You have inspired me with your courage. I am grateful for the opportunity you have given me to grow as a person and a therapist. You are why I wanted to write this book.

To my friends and colleagues; I am the beneficiary of your commitment to excellence and your desire to elevate those around you. I am blessed that in one way or another our lives have become woven into the rich tapestry that it is: Patrick Carnes, Stefanie Carnes, Alex Katehakis, Rob Weiss, Belinda Berman-Real, Terry Real, Stan Tatkin, Kelly McDaniel, Anna Valenti-Anderson, Amanda Bird, and Tara Kroeger—thank you!

The Muses were the nine Greek goddesses of literature, science and the arts; their gifts inspired musicians and writers to reach greater artistic and intellectual heights. Properly speaking, a muse is a female or refers to a feminine force. I want to acknowledge Michael Lewis,

Aaron Sorkin, and Colson Whitehead. They are my modern-day muses; each is a writing powerhouse in his own right. To invoke these three acclaimed male writers as my inspiration is an unexpected, but fitting, role-reversal of Greek mythology.

There are the angels we meet, by design or by accident, who help us along the way. My angels are Jill Arzouman, Julie Klewer, Tracy Barnett, Jennifer Schneider, Libby Timmons, Dena Baumgartner, Rae Soobratty, Debra Milner, Param Dedhia, Josh Raynor, and Deb Lazarus. We have traveled many miles together; I look forward to traveling many more.

Finally, I'd like to thank my family. *Battle of the Titans* and its eponymous chapter would not be the same without their contributions. My mother provided me an unexpected gift by sharing so openly about herself and her marriage. Thank you, Mom. Jonah, Jared and Risa; I am grateful for your love and support. You each inspire me, just by being yourselves—I love you.

FOREWORD

In 2013, my friend and colleague Debra Kaplan published *For Love and Money: Exploring Sexual & Financial Betrayal in Relationships*. Prior to that work, the phrase "relationship betrayal" was mostly relegated to the interpersonal trauma of sexual and romantic infidelity. *For Love and Money* burst that particular bubble by explaining how sexual, romantic, and financial betrayal are often linked. That book accurately noted the painful emotional trauma that occurs when one intimate partner holds on to a secret and hidden agenda (financial, sexual, romantic, etc.) while the other is left unaware, uninformed, and uninvolved. This meaningful concept that both Debra and I embrace explains how relational infidelity can appear in non-sexual forms. Thus, we view infidelity as occurring whenever one partner purposefully keeps important secrets from the other for personal benefit.

Having set the stage with *For Love and Money*, Debra now offers, in *Battle of the Titans*, a deeper dive into the dynamic power struggles that couples can unhappily play out related to both sex and money.

Without question, all relationships must inevitably deal with power imbalances. Whether it's parent-child, boss-worker, or lovers/spouses, in any given situation one person generally has the upper hand in some way. But this is not a bad thing. Being able to negotiate in and out of power imbalances with good communication and boundaries can make us stronger. A boss must lead his or her employees, and the employees must deliver what is asked. A parent must educate and model healthy living for his or her child, and the child must learn. And if handled fairly and openly, most healthy, mutually supportive relationships will move in and out of these dynamics with care and empathy toward others.

That said, in healthy, strong, mutually enjoyable relationships, there is a give and take with this power dynamic. Bosses should always value the feedback and suggestions their employees offer them. And while parents often oversee the decisions made by their children, every child should still feel that his or her beliefs and opinions matter. With transparency and open communication, such relationship dynamics are mutually beneficial without one person leaving the other feeling controlled, smothered, or taken advantage of.

Unfortunately, this type of relationship give-and-take is not always present. And when it's not there, or not there often enough, there will be strife. Whenever two or more people are committed to a particular goal, the parties involved will struggle to be heard, to be right, and to have the upper hand. In short, they will struggle for power within the relationship. This is human nature.

Nowhere is this dynamic more obvious than when money and sex enter the equation. The #MeToo movement, for example, has been lifted to international prominence related to powerful, wealthy men abusing both money and power to obtain sex and to then keep their predatory behaviors under wraps. Often, such behaviors continued for years or even decades, despite countless complaints, payoffs, and the "open secret" nature of their actions. Such men were reassured by the belief that money, position, and power would keep them safe and in control. And we all have publicly witnessed the outcome of these types of arrogant and narcissistic choices and beliefs.

Of course, most of us did not need to watch the #MeToo movement unfold to know that money and sex have been a form of relational currency since humans first evolved. To this point, it's useful to keep in mind that throughout history, most marriages, until fairly recently, were considered to be more of a financial choice than a decision based on romantic attachment. Back in the day, couples were paired up (often by parents and others in power) for survival, the growth of the family, or factors related to politics, religion, and wealth. Yes, we humans are driven to pair bond, but this natural drive toward connection has historically been (and continues to be) exploited for personal, financial, familial, and political gain.

Without question, the money, sex, and power dynamic still exists. Research tells us that conflicts about money are one of the greatest predictors of divorce in the 21st century. So the money/sex power struggle is (and always has been) a volatile source of conflict, the impact of which can be greatly amplified by an individual's past trauma, issues with self-worth, interpersonal fears, and related emotional challenges.

Debra Kaplan's extensive Wall Street and clinical experience makes her the perfect professional to deliver this information. To this end, *Battle of the Titans* offers a carefully organized, thoughtful focus on the facts, ideas, and concepts utilized to identify and work through intimate power differentials, while supporting each individual to focus on self-healing and empathy toward how others experience them. By following the guidance outlined in this book, couples can learn to establish mutually acceptable and beneficial relationship boundaries. Healing relationships by examining and aligning a couple's shared goals creates a roadmap of mutuality and awareness that serves anyone who respects and is committed to one another. With this useful guidance, couples can learn to value and respect not only their own relational currency, but also that of their partner. In this way, *Battle of the Titans* lays out the path toward more stable and engaged intimacy in 21st century relationships.

ROBERT WEISS, Ph.D., LCSW
Chief Clinical Officer,
Seeking Integrity Treatment Programs

INTRODUCTION

POWER

*Knowing others is intelligence; knowing yourself
is true wisdom. Mastering others is strength;
mastering yourself is true power.*

— Lao-Tzu

This book is about power. More specifically, it is about learning how to master the forces of sex, money, and power in your relationships. Few of us ever want to be powerless. And yet, as humans, we are destined to feel powerless at many points in our lives especially when we are in intimate relationships.

Sex and money are two "currencies" that humans wield for ultimate power, control and exploitation. An imbalance of sex and money can play out across cultures and demographics. No one socioeconomic cohort—profession, personality type, gender, ethnicity, sexual orientation, age, education level, or identity, has cornered the market on sexual or financial exploitation. The battle for power and control is universal and omnipresent in society. Contrary to popular belief, power struggles about sex and money occur even in the healthiest of relationships. It's the human condition.

POWER IN RELATIONSHIPS

I became fascinated with the concept of power from a young age when I watched my parents' fights. Their marital spats and arguments about money were legendary, but my eventual power struggles with my father became herculean. I held significant influence in their marriage. This dynamic forged my tenacious character and propelled me into professions that celebrated strength but more importantly—rewarded power. The ultimate pay off.

On Wall Street money is the spoils of war, but power is the fiat currency—an unofficial medium of exchange, often held in higher esteem than money itself. I observed power and control in those who competed for financial success and accolade. Those I'm referring to included me. Had I not been drawn to power from a young age, I would not have pursued a career in business, nor would I have pursued and procured several highly coveted positions at Wall Street firms. Such a calling card conveyed elite influence.

Nowadays, as a psychotherapist, I derive infinitely more pleasure and satisfaction from a very different and more valued form of power: helping clients successfully resolve their relationship power struggles that have become an all-consuming and driving force toward misery and destruction. The competition I observe today is in the push-pull between romantic partners about sex and money.

Couples therapy is often difficult work, and because of that, many therapists choose to specialize only with individuals. It is because of my power struggles with my father and what I observed in my parents' marriage that I am drawn to couples work. Those experiences directly impacted me as a person and a therapist. Navigating power struggles in business was complicated but therapy work is more complex since the dynamics aren't just sexual, but financial as well. The relational stakes are higher and at times downright ruinous to the relationship. Unbeknownst to me, I had trained for this challenge my whole life, and it is also the reason I wanted to write this book.

Until 2013, when I published *For Love and Money: Exploring Sexual & Financial Betrayal in Relationships* (herein referred to as *For Love and Money*), much had been written about sex, and much had been written about money, but very little had been written about the ways that sex and money intersect in relationships. My hope was that *For Love and Money* offered the reader a unique and forward-thinking perspective into sexual, financial and relational exploitation with an emphasis on sexual addiction.

For Love and Money was very helpful for those who were involved in an addictive relationship or sexual and financial betrayal, but beyond addiction, many more couples experience unhealthy or exploitive dynamics. In session after session, I helped couples whose arguments were mired in sexual and financial power dynamics. This phenomenon isn't just a concern for the modern relationship. Power has fascinated humans since the dawn of time. It was the life force of ancient Greek mythology.

I began to think about how my personal and professional experiences with power could benefit my clients. I knew that couples had much to gain by exploring power dynamics through the triple lens of personal insights, Greek myth, and the language of therapy.

I wanted to write a book to provide couples tools to establish sexual and financial balance in relationships. More important than that, I wanted to help people prevent exploitative abuse in their intimate relationships. This quest became more urgent in light of unfolding world events in which I saw my life and my clients' experiences reflected.

Thus, The *Battle of the Titans* was born.

WHAT'S AHEAD

In this book we will explore power dynamics in relationships using that triple lens, digging into myth, personal stories, and the language of therapy. I will share tools with you, that I have shared with my clients, to establish sexual and financial balance.

The fact that power differentials exist is not in question. How couples navigate them is. Therefore, we will explore the science of power and psychological principles to strengthen ourselves and our intimate relationships to see precisely how we empower or disempower ourselves. This book will help you navigate those complex dynamics. You'll also learn to establish a healthy balance of power in your relationship by exploring how power can be negotiated in family and adult dynamics.

Chapter One will survey power across the social, financial and political landscapes. In order for change to occur it is essential to get a different perspective. To fully understand relationships is to bear witness to historical events of its greatest paradox: power. We gain power and the capacity for influence through social practices that advance the interests of others. And yet, once we gain power, success, or wealth, those very practices vanish, leaving us vulnerable to impulsive, self-serving behaviors that set in motion abuse of others, and our ultimate fall.[1]

Chapter Two introduces the golden strands of Greek mythology and personal narrative that are woven throughout the subsequent chapters.

Chapter Three will explore early attachment, both child and adult attachment styles. Learning how we come to overvalue or undervalue our self-worth is vitally important in this journey.

Chapter Four builds on the attachment themes of self-worth and explores the emotional and psychological foundations that contribute to our over- or undervaluation of self and other in relationships.

Chapters Five and *Six* examine the complexities of power and control, narcissism, sexual rage, and shame, and how they are wielded as weapons of abuse. Most essential is an exploration of The Dark Triad, a psychological construct that refers to three personality traits: narcissism, Machiavellianism—a person who utilizes manipulation, self-interest and deception for personal gain—and psychopathy. This construct helps illuminate an exploration into sexual anger, "Eroticized Rage," and financial rage – coined "Monetized Rage." Understanding sexual and financial rage as weapons for power and control are essential factors to safely assess the sexual and financial costs of a relationship.

Chapter Seven will provide you with knowledge and tools to establish new boundaries for yourself and your relationships. We'll explore the various ways that sex and money are exchanged in power dynamics – coined "relational currency." Included in this chapter are tools to establish healthy boundaries so that you can build a balanced and reciprocal relationship.

I knew that in order to experience change in a relationship, I needed to examine it from a different perspective. That action meant that I had to take a proverbial step outside of the relationship in order to examine it more clearly, and if necessary—learn how to empower myself without disempowering another.

When it is appropriate, I share those personal and professional insights with my clients. In these pages I share them with you. Many couples are successful in reframing their relationship dynamics. You can do the same. This book is your path forward.

BATTLE OF THE TITANS

CHAPTER ONE

PUTTING POWER IN PERSPECTIVE

Be not the slave of your own past – plunge into
the sublime seas, dive deep, and swim far, so you
shall come back with new self-respect, with
new power, and with an advanced experience
that shall explain and overlook the old.

— Ralph Waldo Emerson

Perspective is everything. We use it to understand ourselves and relate to the world around us, but perspective also requires context. Without it we lack or lose the significance or meaning in which to consider our perspective.

As a female working on Wall Street, my experience gave me a unique perspective into that white, male-dominated world. One doesn't have to work on Wall Street or be a therapist to understand how the intersection of power and control might play out in relationships, because off Wall Street and outside of politics, evidence of power is everywhere.

My time on Wall Street brought the point home and my time as a client and now a therapist has merely reinforced the idea. Early in my business career, I worked in banking before I left to study for an MBA. I returned to Wall Street and worked for a large brokerage firm before

I began trading commodity options on the Coffee, Sugar, and Cocoa Exchange and the New York Futures Exchange located in the World Trade Center.

HOW TO SUCCEED IN BUSINESS...AS A FEMALE

When I was an option trader in the commodity pits, women comprised a small percentage of the total number of traders. I arrived armed with validating degrees but more to the point, the confidence that I deserved a proverbial seat at the table. I had much, if not more to offer than some of my male colleagues.

This was the late 80s and greed and excess were in full display. The environment on Wall Street was at times like a frat house. Lavish parties, trips, and extravagant dinners were the norm. I wasn't excluded; I wasn't interested in partaking in the antics.

Back in those days many foreign banks were located in midtown Manhattan. The French bank I worked for was located in Rockefeller Center. Our offices towered over the tourist district which was both exciting and frustrating. Getting from one place to another might involve pushing through long, snaking queues or throngs of tourists, depending on the time of year. One summer day I noticed impromptu meetings were happening during lunch. There didn't seem to be a specific pattern to the meetings. On some days, men seemed to quickly convene with little notice; on other days, there was an all-out sprint to a meeting room. What, I wondered, could be so urgent? I soon found out that The Radio City Music Hall Rockettes were sunbathing topless on the roof of Radio City

Music Hall, and several of our offices had a towering and uninterrupted view.

Uncouth or crass as my male colleagues' behavior was, my femininity was my strength, and being a woman in a mostly male world offered me certain advantages. I tacitly understood and capitalized on the fact that many male colleagues expected me to lean on sexual guile or a feigned helplessness to get ahead. But I wasn't interested in hustling for approval. I wanted to earn respect. To do that I knew that I had to work harder at my job than my male counterparts for a place at the table, and I did.

Earning respect looked different depending on where I worked. The world of open outcry trading, for example, was a dog-eat-dog world in the commodity pits. Respect in that environment meant that all trades were honored even if the market conditions following a winning trade turned negative. Every trade and every trader had to keep their word if they wanted to be taken seriously and respected on the floor. Wall Street may be sexist but when it came to making money, no one cared where it came from. All that mattered was that it was green. Where money went, power flowed.

Beyond Wall Street, sex and money are points of contention and a power struggle for many reasons, not the least of which are issues of attachment, unresolved trauma, or shame. At the core of this complex dynamic are our learned experiences involving sex, whether that is overt sexual abuse or covert sexual abuse, as was the case for me. The role that money played in one's family of origin will add another layer of complexity to this already intricate tapestry of life. All the accumulation of money in the world or great sex cannot erase insecurities forged in childhood. It will only amplify them.

Our early life experiences form the lens through which we view our self-worth. If we grew up with inadequate empathy and unfulfilled needs in childhood, we will experience this disconnection from emotional safety as shame, guilt, doubt, and low self-esteem. A chronic lack of attunement or even of good enough parenting[1] forges a psychological emptiness. It is the metaphorical hole in the soul. Many will try to compulsively pursue a cycle of self-destructive behaviors: sexual excess, financial risk-taking, and moral superiority. Left to their natural progression, compulsive behaviors ultimately fall short, necessitating a need for even greater levels of psychological reward. Ultimately, it's in an all-out effort to mask the inner void—the core belief that one is inherently unworthy.

HELL HATH NO FURY LIKE A WOMAN SCORNED

Tarana Burke was a youth camp director in Brooklyn, NY, working with survivors of sexual violence in the 90s. In 2007, she began a movement that she called "Me Too," primarily focused on communities of color, in which survivors connected with one another through empathy. She established communities for victims in near obscurity until 2017, when the actor Alyssa Milano stumbled on the phrase, unaware of its origins, and pressed survivors of sexual aggression to use it. The #MeToo movement came to life.

The #MeToo movement captured the zeitgeist. It gave voice to the silenced and gave victims a platform to share their stories of emotional, physical, and sexual abuse. As a therapist I navigate these volatile waters. I'm trained to confront abuse of all types in hopes of shifting a victim into action potential and toward self-empowerment, while reducing the emotional or psychological drivers of the abuse. What underlies this power dynamic has much to do with how each person sees themselves in relation to the other.

These newsworthy headlines careened their way into people's lives. Women and men began to voice their discounted or self-denied pain. Slowly, conversations sprang up in my therapy office as individuals and couples revealed previously denied abuse and exploitation. Numerous female clients shared that they had never discussed their past sexual abuse with their partners. This opened the floodgates to explore how their painful admissions impacted their relationships. Once the groundswell broke, my clients wanted to share their experiences with their partner or spouse but were afraid to do so.

THE IMPACT OF #MeToo ON THERAPY

I understand why people bury the horror of their history under layers of denial so thick that it never sees the light of day, but news events such as these exhume the memories and send them rocketing to the fore. The collective public outrage of the #MeToo movement galvanized some of my clients' strength and courage.

For many victims, the public validation of their private and discounted pain was enough to empower them into action. That action meant casting off the perpetrator's shame and assigning it back where it belonged—with their abuser. Other clients had a more difficult reckoning. The public news forced their denial to the surface, but in their case, action meant sharing their secrets with their partners, reclaiming their lost selves, and building a healthier sexual relationship with their loved one.

At times, the reasons for a couple's sexual dissatisfaction can be explained by the denial of past abuse. I cannot and should not push a client into an admission that isn't their truth, which they may not be ready to address. The #MeToo movement galvanized some clients' strength and courage by way of collective public outrage.

At the time of this writing many more cases of alleged abuse of power are coming to light involving sexual assault, rape, and misconduct. Abuse will always be an element of human interaction. Financial insecurity creates a vulnerable predisposition for control and exploitation, much like a wound that creates an opening for infection. In other words, when money is scarce, there's a greater potential for abuse or exploitation.

The #MeToo Movement was fueled by celebrities who confirmed the existence of Hollywood's worst-kept secret: if you want to succeed in the entertainment business, check your personhood at the door and collude with the system of exploitation ruled by the powerful.

In the spring of 2015, Harvey Weinstein admitted to groping a woman without her consent. His admission was overheard by officers and caught on tape, but it was still not enough for prosecutors to bring charges against him. Despite more than 100 women who came forward with allegations of sexual misconduct and assault, at that time their allegations were not enough to bring a case against Weinstein to trial. Almost five years later Weinstein was finally brought to trial on Feb. 24, 2020. *The Wall Street Journal* reported the findings: "After nearly 20 hours of deliberation following a six-week trial in New York City, the jury found Mr. Weinstein guilty of first-degree criminal sexual act and third-degree rape, and acquitted him of first-degree rape and predatory sexual assault. He faces between five and 25 years in prison on the criminal sexual-act charge and up to four years for third-degree rape."

SEX WITHOUT CONSENT

Where is the line between what is cold, cruel and abusive and what is illegal? Despite how those who create and uphold the law would like to portray it, the legal definition of rape is far from clear. Proving rape in a court of law requires a near herculean effort. The vast majority of cases involve victims who are reluctant to go forward in a "he said, she said" scenario when there is no third-party witness. At other times, victims don't want to relive the assault which is revisited over and over throughout legal proceedings, especially when they are trying to move on with their lives.

Further from public court proceedings are the behind-closed-doors sexual encounters that involve assault between married partners or those in committed relationships. Over the years, I have worked with several individuals and couples who have shared stories of sexual "intimacy," which sound eerily close to sexual abuse or assault. Sexual assault is sex without consent. In these cases, I help the client to understand what consent is and is not, as well as what mutually respectful sexual behavior involves.

Katie Edwards is a professor at the University of Nebraska-Lincoln and the director of the Interpersonal Violence Research Laboratory in the Nebraska Center for Research on Children, Youth, Families and Schools. She knows about sexual assault and intimate partner violence all too well. Her lab researches "young women who remain in relationships with men who sexually assault them. 'It's not uncommon to see sexual assault happen in the context of onging relationships, whether it's colleagues, dating or friends.'"[2]

When exploitation involves sex or money as a weapon, the element of shame must be addressed. Victims report feeling stupid or naive for having not seen the signs of exploitation or betrayal. "Being a trusting, loving, and compassionate person is not shameful behavior," I remind my clients who have suffered such betrayal. "Exploiting someone's trust, love, and compassion is."

On top of the painful self-indictment abuse survivors experience, they may also be subject to public scrutiny that serves up an even more incriminating judgment—the false claim that the victim is somehow to blame because it "takes two to tango" or "knew what they were getting into." Public criticism and victim-shaming become the deeper wounds to endure, particularly when the perpetrator (including those who collude in the abuse) claims the victim role. This is certainly what played out in some of the high-profile cases that surfaced out of Hollywood. What is at play is the confluence of narcissism and abuse of power.

NARCISSISTS AND POWER

Narcissists operate with a sense of entitlement to power. Understanding narcissism is essential to identifying the presence of abuse or control in a relationship. If money and sex are introduced into that equation, the potential for abuse or criminal behavior rises exponentially. Researchers from the University of Melbourne probed the connection between power and narcissism. They found that under certain circumstances narcissists do rise to—and abuse— positions of power. Their research "points to the possibility that structural positions of power and individual differences in narcissism may be mutually reinforcing, suggesting a vicious cycle with personal, relational, and societal implications."[3]

WALL STREET SIDESTEPS ITS #METOO MOMENT

There is a strong potential for exploitation in the deep waters of sex, money, and power. Yet, there was only a deafening silence that emanated from Wall Street while the #MeToo movement was having its run. Although many other titans of their respective professional kingdoms were toppled for sexual misconduct, Wall Street appeared to be immune from the defenestration. Long believed to be a male dominion, financial industries had not had any of their own exposed on the front pages of print media nor skewered in the feeds of social media. How could this be? As the adage goes, "if it seems too good to be true, it probably is."

According to a survey of over 1,000 men and women across the financial services industry in banking, capital markets, financial services, investment banking, and investment management in the U.S.,[4] "Women account for less than 17 percent of senior leaders in investment banking. In private equity, women comprise only 9 percent of senior executives and only 18 percent of total employees, according to a 2017 report by Preqin. At hedge funds and private debt firms, the numbers are similarly low—women hold just 11 percent of leadership roles."[5] The survey conducted in the United States also found that "Nearly two-thirds of women polled say females are less likely than males to reach leadership roles. Only 56 percent of men and 37 percent of women agree that males and females are equally likely to become leaders in their industry."[6]

The significance of these statistics is that the gender disparity that existed on Wall Street made the system blind to its own implicit and explicit sexual harassment—whereby little would be done to change it, if exposed. For instance, a president or CEO will tap loyal friends and colleagues to insulate them and the corporate culture from external inquiry and investigation.

After multiple women accused Les Moonves, former CEO at CBS, of sexual misconduct, Moonves remained at CBS and avoided public scrutiny. It was only after several bombshell reports of women who were about to go public with their allegations that the board censured their CEO and allowed further investigation into the abuse. One allegation of abuse should be enough to sound an alarm, but it took over 30 allegations and the imminent threat of public exposure of the abuse before the board took action to investigate.

So how is it that not a single male executive finds himself outed in the sexual harassment scandal crosshairs? Perhaps because there is no exploitation happening and that is why there is little noise coming from the powerful men who dominate the C-suite (CEO, CFO, CIO, COO) stratum of Wall Street. So wrote Thornton McEnery, Executive editor for Dealbreaker.com: "It's a huge relief to divine from the absence of examples [of abuse] that chivalry is indeed the dominating behavior on today's trading floors, and that hedge funds are the temples of Wokeness that we always assumed them to be. We always kind of knew in our heart-of-hearts that female first year analysts at investment banks were treated like queens, but it's so nice to be able to surmise it to be true."[7]

Wall Street had received an early wakeup call in the late '90s when 23 women sued a brokerage firm for sexual harassment and pay discrimination. The class action lawsuit became known as the "Boom-Boom Room" suit, named after the firm's basement party room. Though nearly 2,000 women joined the case, exposing Wall Street's testosterone-driven culture, the motivation was short-lived. While other institutions fell in line and initiated changes to promotion and pay disparities, on Wall Street the barriers that kept women from obtaining senior management roles persisted, and limitations were put in place to keep female employees from seeking damages in court.[8] The #MeToo movement that was destined for Hollywood did little to usher Wall Street toward lasting change.

The silence was later broken in late March 2018, when a judge in the U.S. District Court, Southern District of New York handed down a decision for 2,300 current and former female employees of Goldman Sachs Group, Inc. The female associates and vice presidents who worked in Goldman's investment banking, investment management, and securities divisions since September 2004 accused Goldman Sachs of discriminating against them in pay, promotions and performance reviews. The judge's decision gave them the legal right to pursue their claims as a group in a class action lawsuit.

Wall Street is undoubtedly full of #MeToo survivors. In the past several years more women have begun to occupy senior leadership positions, but essential to enduring change is the need for diversity that has yet to occur. Women and diverse populations continue to be underrepresented in senior leadership at every level. Sexual harassment is known to flourish in organizations where few women hold core positions, or where they have little authority to make executive decisions.

POWER PARADOXES:
THE LIGHT AT THE END OF THE TUNNEL

The German word *schadenfreude* means "the pleasure that one feels from another person's misfortune" and is apt for individuals who exploit, control and revel in the power and control they wield over others. With the rise of social media, it seems that as a society we are becoming more self-promoting or self-centered. We enjoy those whose meteoric rise—and equally calamitous fall are in the public eye.

Dacher Keltner is the director of the Berkeley Social Interaction Laboratory at the University of California, Berkeley, and the author of *The Power Paradox: How We Gain and Lose Influence*. Keltner studies power and its paradoxes—for example, those at the top "may be the very people most blind to the problems of powerlessness, poverty, and inequality"—even if they mean well. According to Keltner's research, individuals who acquire greater power tend to exhibit increasing levels of greed, deceit, sexual violence, or plain old arrogance. His research also speaks to the notion that power contains the seeds of its own destruction.

Our prognosis appears bleak.

Gratefully, Keltner's studies also reveal a counterintuitive message: those who choose not to hoard power, but rather to share it, experience a correlating rise in self-respect and empathy. We build our own self-empowerment in ways that connect and bring us together rather than divide and separate us.

Social psychology research shows that when we engage in altruistic or prosocial acts of service for others, inspire gratitude, and collaborate with those around us, our compassion grows. This psychological principle underscores another powerful paradox: when we give and thus experience ourselves as givers, we increase our self-esteem and receive a more enduring affirmation in our connection to others.

The Social Psychology of Power (Guinote, & Vescio, 2010) is a comprehensive and near-exhaustive review of classic and contemporary research. Within its text leading experts review, "evolutionary bases of power; its effects on physiological processes, cognitive abilities, and health; what sorts of people are given power; when, how, and whom power corrupts; and power dynamics in gender, social class, and ethnic relations."[9]

A powerful example of the social psychologists' research was found in the strength and collaboration of social advocacy immediately following President Donald J. Trump's inauguration. Worldwide protests advocating for women's rights and immigration reform erupted as a political response, reflecting what studies on empathy show: that emotionally intelligent, connected and empathetic people ultimately rise higher in the ranks of power. The Women's Marches of January 21, 2017 were the largest and most peaceful one-day protests in modern U.S. history.

The interweave of power and control may be the purview of social psychologists, but these golden strands are the Greek mythological story of the Moirae—the three goddesses of fate who, at the birth of a man, controlled his destiny by spinning out the thread of his future life and directing the consequences of his actions.

While the all-powerful Moirae, or, the Fates—as they are known—controlled the mother thread of life, the Greek mythology family tree originated out of Chaos—the void state preceding the creation of the universe. Gaia originated out of Chaos. We pick up family narratives and Greek mythology in the next chapter.

CHAPTER TWO

Battle of the Titans

Owning our story can be hard but not nearly
as difficult as spending our lives running from it.
Embracing our vulnerabilities is risky but
not nearly as dangerous as giving up on love
and belonging and joy—the experiences
that make us the most vulnerable. Only when we
are brave enough to explore the darkness
will we discover the infinite power of our light.

— Brené Brown

Greek mythology has enthralled human imagination for centuries. Famous for their accounts of world creation and immortal beings who battled for supreme dominance, these myths are essentially stories about power. Any drama that modern-day imagination creates has already played out in these stories.

Infamous among the epic cycles of birth, displacement, and succession is the myth of the Titans, twelve siblings born to primordial parents, Gaia (earth) and Uranus (sky). The Titans were the first generation of children born to these "first" parents and preceded the Olympians who would rule from Mount Olympus.

Uranus was known to be controlling of Gaia and his children. Kronos, the youngest of the twelve siblings, envied his father's power. He was also the only sibling willing to rebel against it. With the help of his mother, he plotted an ambush. When the time was right, Kronos deposed Uranus by castrating him with a scythe provided by his mother. Kronos assumed command of the cosmos and ruled during a period known as the Golden Age. In what would become the classic Greek revenge and succession cycle, Kronos was eventually deposed by his own son, Zeus, in a series of clashes referred to as the Battle of the Titans.

The term "titan" is a reference to these myths. Modern titans are the rich and powerful among us who wield their power to manipulate others. It's also an apt metaphor to describe my relationship with my father.

MY TITANOMACHY

I grew up as the middle of three children. My brother and I arrived approximately two years apart and to my parents' surprise, my sister was conceived seven months after I was born. My father was a successful businessman and my mother stayed at home with the three of us all under the age of four. When I was one year old my parents moved us out of New York City to the suburbs.

According to modern birth order paradigms, middle children are often lost between the oldest, entitled firstborn and the pampered younger sibling. My experience bears out that paradigm as accurate in that my voice was overpowered by those of my brother and sister. My needs took a backseat to theirs. From the middle, back seat of our black Chrysler DeSoto, I had a literal and figurative view into my parents' relationship.

My mother was emotionally unavailable. In truth, she was overwhelmed as a parent. She was unable to provide the real emotional care I needed. In her efforts to help assuage my emotional wounds from friends and bullies, she took me in her arms and delivered a pep talk somewhere between "It can't be that bad" and "Things will get better." I learned that her version of nurturing offered little in the way of emotional support and much in the way of invalidation. She couldn't handle her own emotional needs, much less her children's. She was, however, a fabulous teacher. Teaching was her true passion and she made learning fun. I'm grateful for her tutoring through my toughest elementary school lessons.

My dad, on the other hand, was the more emotionally available parent in whom I could trust, albeit inconsistently. When I needed help coping with my growing insecurities and mounting worry in the world, it was to him that I turned for support. My father didn't realize it, but he intellectualized his feelings, and being that I most closely resembled my father in character and personality, I learned to talk about, but never feel, my own emotions.

I developed a personality based on dichotomies. My budding sense of conviction and determination belied my deeper struggles with self-doubt. I formed expert coping mechanisms while building on a fragile, if not vaporous, inner self, further complicating my distorted identity and developing the double-bind in which I was living.

By definition, a double-bind is a dilemma in which a person is confronted with two competing yet irreconcilable demands. The only resolution to the dilemma is two equally undesirable courses of action. In my case, to survive an intolerable lack of emotional nurturing I became self-sufficient and emotionally needless. I learned a psychological hat trick that all humans consciously or unconsciously employ to exist in uncomfortable circumstances: be supportive to get support. I became, in a sense, my father's spouse and my mother's mother.

These early experiences and observations forged my core beliefs that I still possess today. From my own personal memory and family testament, it's clear that I've always exhibited a strong sense of independence. My genetic predisposition may have influenced my sense of individuality, but growing up in my household implicitly forged my true personality: determined, tenacious, and fragile.

From my middle backseat, I watched my parents fight. My mother was no match for my father. Under his verbal lashing, she quietly seethed and stared out the window.

I loved my parents, but in those moments, I loathed them. I despised my father's searing tongue and contempt for my mother. I despised how she couldn't or wouldn't stand up for herself, preferring to sit in silence and stare out the window to an escape somewhere far away. That escape came to fruition when I was five years old and she began her graduate studies in teaching. She slipped out from under my father's derision into financial independence. My mother found her voice in the classroom, but it wasn't until many years later that she found it in their marriage.

Around the time my mother finished school and became a teacher, my father changed occupations. He started studying for his new career as a therapist. My mother ran from her feelings but my father leaned into his. When I was an adult, my mother shared with me that she delivered him an ultimatum, saying, "If you become a therapist, I'll divorce you." Undaunted by the threat, he did just that.

I watched as my father worked hard to become a therapist while creating an emotional bypass to his past. By all outward appearances, he mastered this leap, but I knew this to be untrue. His outward appearance and inner self were incongruent.

In spite of my mother's ultimatum and my father's noncompliance, they didn't divorce. My parents remained married until my father died shortly after their 50th wedding anniversary. However, their arguments grew more frequent and their marriage more distant. My mother's vacancy in the marriage infuriated my father, and during their years of marital discord my father and I grew close.

Beginning in my adolescence and into my early adulthood, my father frequently confided in me about his discontent and frustration with my mother. I liked this trust and grew to believe that I was the only person who could possibly understand his inter-marital troubles.

Like Kronos, I rose beyond my ordinary status as a child while my siblings remained children. Inwardly, I coveted my role as emotional spouse and confidante. I believe this shift in the family dynamics unconsciously granted my mother license to vacate her role—and at times the home—to pursue her newfound freedom.

However, this "adult" responsibility came at an emotional cost. When my father confided in me, I felt special. I was too young to understand that his behavior, unintentional though it may have been, constituted emotional incest. This enmeshment robbed me of a healthy parent-child relationship. As much as my father needed an appropriate adult partner, I was not that. And as for me, I needed a parent, not a confidante.

THE TITAN REVOLT

The cost of being a golden child surfaced when I was an adolescent and I began to date. I noticed that when I was attracted to someone, strong anxiety erupted. This uneasiness grew more intense when the attraction was reciprocated.

The early phase of romantic human attraction is called limerence—the involuntary human response of being infatuated or obsessed with another. During this natural phase, there is a strong desire for reciprocation of attraction as we are drawn toward this new and novel individual.

However, I found that the longer I spent time with someone, the deeper my inner turmoil became. That turmoil led to disgust as my fears of being ensnared and trapped grew. For example, I was in a relationship during my final year of high school. We had only ever dated each other, even though we both knew that it would end after graduation. This, for me, was tolerable.

One night, he invited me to his house for a family dinner. I had met his parents before, so this was not my first introduction. It was a lovely dinner and I was excited to be the center of attention. As I sat in the spotlight I became overwhelmed by the thought that I was now obligated to this person and his family. After that evening, a panic surfaced in me and an all too familiar cycle was triggered. We broke up shortly thereafter.

As was the case in this relationship, panic intensified into dread until such time that I either a) became critical of the love interest and pushed him away (which provided me relief and a sense of control over my fear), or b) I abruptly ended the connection in order to escape.

I was unnerved. I had no idea what caused my gripping fear. I reasoned that perhaps my partners were too desperate, or that I was attracted to, and was attracting, "weird" people. I was correct but not in the ways I surmised.

To make matters worse, my reaction and the consequent cycle became more engulfing and more bewildering when I was the pursuer and the attention was reciprocated. The fear welled up inside. I tried to ignore it and push it away, but like a tsunami generated by a submerged disruption, my fear created a wave of gripping panic and terror. I became paralyzed by the push/pull and trapped by the double-bind of being simultaneously emotionally hungry and emotionally unavailable.

The "push" resulted from caretaking my father's adult distress and being ill equipped as a child and adolescent to carry his emotional burden.

Being alone in the car, for example, provided an opportunity for us to talk and for my father to vent his distress. I treasured the chance to be in the front seat literally and figuratively. I felt honored to sit in my mother's seat, offering support and solace. Those moments provided me what I was missing; connection. My mother's emotional disconnect deprived me of nurturing and connection—I had nowhere to go with my despair and loneliness. Those private moments with my father drew me closer and into a more incestuous complicity. I took on the wife role. "I understand exactly why you're upset," I'd say.

The "pull" was formed by my insecure yet bottomless need for attention as a result of being cast in an adult role of importance. Children are both an extension and reflection of a parent's love. In a healthy dynamic, a parent will allow the child to grow beyond their self-shadow and become a separate being. This is true, healthy love. Though I had no doubt that my father loved me, as I loved him, I experienced his love as repressive. At times, it felt as if there wasn't enough air in the room or space in the family for us to coexist.

DEPOSING URANUS

It would be years before I understood what was happening in that unhealthy dynamic and many more years before I learned to reconcile my simultaneous fear of closeness and desire for it.

In my personal work, I learned to extricate myself from my father's enmeshment. I deposed my father and took the power that was rightfully mine. I was able to establish clear boundaries around my romantic relationships and limit the information I shared with my father.

I learned to let go of control and create interdependence

in a relationship. For me, I had to find a Goldilocks-esque balance: not too close, not too far, but just right. In essence, I had to reconcile a natural and simultaneous desire for closeness and the need for reciprocal individuality.

I also learned that street smarts rather than book smarts could be my ticket to success. After all, I'd grown up in a household where knowing how to "read the landscape" for mixed messages, emotional traps, and sabotage became instinctual. I owe my success in business and as a therapist to my well-honed gut instinct and intuition.

As a therapist, I help clients work through their relationship struggles. I describe this emotional tension as the intra- (one's own) and inter- (between two) psychic experiences of relationships.

Because of my own history, I relate to my clients and empathize with their struggle. However, being a therapist doesn't make me immune to anxiety, depression, or feeling lonely and alone. Perhaps because my father intellectualized his emotions, and was a therapist—I believed I would be immune from pain. That defense may have protected him, but I was not interested in charade or a therapeutic bypass. These issues were the focus of many years of therapy. I still struggle to find that inter-psychic and intra-psychic sweet spot. Learning to tolerate this distress has been, at times, insurmountable.

FINANCIAL POWER AT PLAY

My parents' struggle, as well as my own power dynamics with my father, underscored the overt and covert strategies people use to wield and exploit power and control. Their marriage taught me about the power of money. As an adolescent, and now as an adult, I have the benefit of historical perspective—my own and my mother's.

As I was writing this book, I spoke with my mother about their marriage. I was reluctant to bring up the topic of their marital discord because my mother has told me she feels tremendous guilt for rejecting my father and his attempts for emotional connection. Instead, I asked about his control in the marriage.

I underestimated my mother's insight into her own marriage.

"You think there was control from only one direction. His need to control me was only part of the picture. He was controlling for sure, but I also put him in a no-win situation."

I was surprised she was so easily admitting to her passive-aggressive behavior.

"I outright refused to take responsibility in our marriage. For example, if your father asked me for ideas about where I think we should go on vacation, I put him off and insisted he just take care of it."

My mother paused in the conversation. I wasn't sure if she was thinking back to the past or if she was overwhelmed by emotion.

"I outright refused to participate in any discussion about finances or even listen to him when he tried to show me where the water shut-off valve was to the house in the case of an emergency. I only found my voice after one particularly nasty fight. Your father always hated paying the bills. We would get into terrible fights because he was so worried about money all the time and questioned me about every purchase or bill."

I couldn't recall the "nasty" fight that she referenced, but I do remember the incessant bickering and sniping between them, especially on the day that my father put aside to pay the bills. This financial ritual was stressful for everyone in the house.

For as long as I can remember, one Sunday afternoon every month, my father put classical music on the stereo and sat at the dining room table to pay the household bills. He laid out the bills across the table and methodically wrote a check for each bill. We were financially comfortable, yet his fear about money was palpable. It emanated like gamma rays throughout the house and plagued him up until the day he died.

His fear of future financial insufficiency was driven by his financial struggles in his childhood. This was an important lesson: the emotional significance of money transcends time and space. Fear can manifest regardless of current financial or relationship status.

I don't ever remember a time that we went without anything—food, clothing or opportunity. We always had enough, yet my father was continually afraid that the money wouldn't last.

I had drifted away and into the past when I realized that my mother was still thinking. "Mom, you were saying?"

"I remember now how the fight started. He was harping on me about a bill for something I purchased. He insisted on knowing why I bought it. I finally screamed at him, 'I earn the money and you have no right to tell me what I can or cannot buy! If you hate seeing what I buy, then why don't I pay the bills!'

"'YES,' he yelled. 'All I've ever wanted was for you to pay the bills! Please!' All he ever wanted was for me to get involved in our finances! He begged me to do so! It was only that day that I found my voice and took over because I became irate and yelled at him to stop trying to control me!"

From that point in time until my father died, my mother paid the bills. She also became the breadwinner and supported the household expenses during the years that my father went back to school and into the early years of his career. My father had supported her financial independence and encouraged her to grow, but that was in juxtaposition to his continued attempts to control her and money. She may have flipped the financial marital script, but the emotional imbalance remained.

My mother laughed at the absurdity of the argument. I realized that I was quiet, lost in thought, and I began to feel angry. Certainly, it wasn't on my father's behalf—I had no interest in taking up his cause and caretaking his emotional needs from beyond the grave. I pondered a bit longer and drilled down into my anger.

The anger seemed to stem from the fact that my mother was now willing to acknowledge my father's needs in death; having unconsciously denied them in life.

Then came my stark recognition. Blind to her own behavior, she also denied me my needs as a child. Only in recent years has my mother been emotionally present. She has never acknowledged her emotional unavailability in my youth.

I was becoming furious. Ironically, I was the one who had a hard time staying present. I had anticipated neither the conversation nor the emotional upheaval I was now feeling. I was also a bit shaken by my mother's vivid recall of the events. It was so out of character for her to remember details of her own life in this way, and I wasn't sure where this conversation would lead.

INTERRUPTING FAMILY PATTERNS

As I write this, my mother is 90 years old and is mentally sharp as a tack. Age aside, her recollection of events both recent and historical has always been a challenge. I attribute this memory deficit to the fact that she was emotionally disconnected at the time. It's hard to recall events never imprinted into memory.

It was important to me that my mother knew that I would be including my personal recollections about their marriage in this book. Every day is one more day that I have with her and I am grateful. Before this conversation, I didn't think to ask nor invite my mother to offer her personal perspective about her marriage. I am sad to admit that it had not occurred to me because I didn't think she had the self-awareness to do so.

Over the years, my mother has become more able or willing to connect with me. Perhaps her age has made her more reflective, but this is sad and frustrating. My mother never listened and now that she is, she can barely hear.

I was uneasy but resolute about where I wanted to take our conversation. Although I was concerned that my mother would not do well with emotionally pointed discussions, I wanted to know the extent to which my mother knew about my father and his emotional incest of me, or if she knew at all.

In many ways, my curiosity put my mother in a no-win position. If she admitted, "Yes, I knew," and showed awareness of my father's enmeshment and inappropriate sharing, she'd be culpable for emotionally abandoning me.

If she answered, "No, I didn't know," then she was by default acknowledging that she was an absent mother and wife, and might have to grapple with the reality of that abandonment.

Either way, the answer might prompt some painful introspection for her and that is never an easy path to confront.

It was in the spirit of love, respect (and admittedly some frustration), that I nervously turned our conversation to the topic.

"Did you understand what was happening between Dad and me?"

"What do you mean?"

"Did you know that for years, Dad turned to me to share his frustration and discontent about you and the marriage?"

"No, I didn't know that. I knew you were close and that the two of you were very similar. Compared to your sister or brother you were the one most like your father in character and personality. I thought that was the reason you both butted heads when you were older and early on in your marriage."

I held my breath as she spoke. I was sad and embarrassed for my mother, and I didn't really know where to go from there. I suppose there was nowhere to go—no amount of clarifying could explain years of denial.

So, there it was, the middle path of two potential outcomes. Her recollection of the family dynamics conveyed neither awareness nor intentional avoidance. In truth, the only reality that matters is that I was emotionally abandoned by both parents simply because neither was present to nurture me in the ways that I needed. My middle path is to parent my inner child as she needed—I can think of no better parent than me.

If the reality that matters is that I was emotionally abandoned, the bigger reality is that family dynamics are complicated and, at times, fraught with conflict. This turmoil can shape a family system for generations to come.

After Kronos took the throne and became ruler of the Universe, his parents Uranus and Gaia made a dire prediction: Kronos' own children would rebel against him and end his rule, just as he'd done. To avoid that fate, Kronos swallowed each of his children whole when they were born.

Rhea, his sister-wife, was alarmed. She tricked Kronos and hid her youngest, Zeus, in a cave in Crete, thus saving him from his father's murderous paranoia. Thus the prophecy came to pass. Like his father before him, Kronos had become a tyrant destined for deposing.

When Zeus grew up, he led his siblings in a rebellion against their father in the period known as the Titanomachy, the great war that occurred between the Titans.

My mother believed the conflict between my father and me was due to our similarities. Certainly, that contributed to our clashes—we both have strong personalities.

Our conflict eventually grew to mythic proportions.

I refused to repeat the generational cycle that held a prophecy for my children. I was aware that to interrupt this dynamic and save myself, as well as my future children, I would have to escape from under his enmeshment. My revolt led to a rupture that divided our family for many years to come.

*

CHAPTER THREE

OUR FAMILY – THE POWER
OF HUMAN ATTACHMENT

*It would be easy to make fun of all this
primate behavior if not for the fact that our
fellow simians take the pursuit of power
and sex just as seriously as we do.*

— Frans de Waal
Dutch primatologist and ethologist

Gaia epitomizes power and creativity. She was the
first deity to have been formed out of Chaos—the
origin of everything, and the symbol of motherhood and
fertility. She was so powerful that she parthenogenetically
birthed Uranus, whom she later married, and with whom
she birthed many children. Uranus disliked most of their
progeny and considered all of them threats to his power.
Uranus was so repelled by the sight of three of the children,
the Hecatoncheires, that he tried to push them back into a
hidden place of the earth, namely Gaia's womb. Hurt and
enraged at Uranus for his cruelty, Gaia plotted to overthrow
him with the help of her son, Kronos.

Gaia was neither meek nor subservient to Uranus.
She was the personification of life itself, a providing and

encouraging mother. Gaia's motivation was to protect her children, so much so that she was willing to wield her power at the expense of her husband's rule.

In the modern world, mothers are still the primary parent with whom most children form their first attachments. An infant's initiation with power and powerlessness begins at birth with a mother/child connection. Self-worth begins with the process of infant attachment and bonding and grows out of these primary relationships with our parents. The attachment experience influences all subsequent relationships in our lives.

PAIR-BONDING AND ATTACHMENT

The bonding process is not exclusive to humans. The evolutionary process is representative of all mammalian mother/infant pair bonds and is vital for an offspring's normal behavioral and social development. Bonding begins during pregnancy and is the biological process by which a mother connects or attaches to her child. It is strongest in human mother/infant pairs. While bonding is the emotional connection experienced by the mother or material figure with the child, it eventually widens to include an expanding circle of caregivers.

Attachment theory, which I address in greater detail in the Addendum at the end of this book, is a psychological model to describe the dynamics of short and long-term interpersonal relationships between humans. Attachment and bonding are complementary processes involved in human connection. Attachment is a reciprocal and mutual process between parent and child. It also speaks to how the child connects with the caregiver. Bonding is the emotional connection and closeness that a mother feels toward her child.

Expectant parents anxiously await their newborn's arrival, and when they meet, fall into a state of ecstasy and love. John Bowlby, a British psychoanalyst, was one of the first to describe attachment as the process of bonding between human beings.

"A mother is likely during the next few days to spend many hours just looking at her new possession, cuddling him, and getting to know him. Usually there comes a moment when she feels the baby is her very own. For some it comes early, perhaps when she first holds him or when he first looks into her eyes. For a large minority of infants who are delivered in hospital, however, it may be delayed for up to a week, often until they are home again (Robson and Kumar 1980)."[1]

This back and forth pair gazing between mother and child biologically initiates the process of continued bonding and attachment. Our earliest connections established with a primary caregiver or others in a family system become part of the ever-expanding web of human social connections.

Studies involving the vocal interchange, or parroting between mother and child, have been shown to establish both the maternal-infant bond at a preverbal level as well as the infant's awareness of self in relationship to another. Long before our ability to form words or the appearance of words, the pattern of turn-taking, which is characteristic of human conversation, takes shape. However healthy or dysfunctional our family of origin may be, we are entirely dependent on them for every need. Without our earliest caregivers, we would not experience a consistent reflection by which we internalize and consequently establish a sense of existence and being. There would be no "here," here.

It is important to note that no caregiver is perfect. Even the most loving and doting parents will eventually misattune to an infant such that the infant's efforts at communication and expression are not responded to satisfactorily. Caregivers learn to manage and repair these breaks in attunement, thus establishing a level of emotional safety for the infant and child. This is how an attachment style is formed.

In my own childhood, I often felt unseen and emotionally vulnerable. Though not physically abandoned, I was emotionally abandoned. Unconsciously, I took the parent reins from my mother. Since I couldn't get her to nurture me, I learned to nurture her so that she could attend to me. I became my mother's mother.

EMOTIONAL CO-REGULATING

Two names synonymous with psychological attachment theory are the aforementioned John Bowlby along with Mary D. Salter Ainsworth. Bowlby described attachment as, "a lasting psychological connectedness between human beings."[2] According to Bowlby's theory, infants rely on their caregivers, who become the child's perceived safe haven and eventual partner for emotional co-regulation. When the caregiver is emotionally healthy and available, an infant will experience comfort and learns to attach securely.

Bowlby further proposed that children are motivated by a primordial need to seek proximity and comfort from caregiver figures in times of distress. Caregivers who are consistently available and responsive during times of distress are fundamental in creating a safe haven from which a child can explore the world and begin the process of safely and securely forming other attachments.

"According to Bowlby, a motivational system, what he called the attachment behavioral system, was gradually 'designed' by natural selection to regulate proximity to an attachment figure."[3] As such, Bowlby delineated four key elements:

- *Secure Base*: A caregiver provides a consistent presence from which the child can explore the world.
- *Safe Haven*: When in distress, a child returns to the caregiver for comfort and soothing.
- *Proximity Maintenance*: The child attempts to stay near the caregiver, thus assuring safety.
- *Separation Distress*: When separated from the caregiver, a child will become upset and distressed.

Mary D. Salter Ainsworth was an American-Canadian developmental psychologist best known for her work with caregiver infant dyads. Her contributions were essential to the field of attachment theory.

Ainsworth joined Bowlby's research team as a mentor and, eventually, an equal partner. Together, they developed what we know today as Attachment Theory, which remains fundamental to our understanding of the psychological distress of an infant when separated from their parents.

STRANGE SITUATION

We define attachment as, "an affectional tie that one person or animal forms between himself and another specific one—a tie that binds them together in space and endures over time."[4] Ainsworth and Bowlby were collaborators, but Ainsworth worked independently and eventually expanded on Bowlby's findings, most notably with an experimental procedure called the "Strange Situation."[5]

In this experiment, a researcher observes a child's reactions when its mother briefly leaves the child alone in an unfamiliar room. The Strange Situation study led Ainsworth to develop her theory with three identified core attachment styles: **Secure, Anxious-Ambivalent,** and **Anxious-Avoidant**.

A child with a **Secure** attachment style becomes upset when his or her caregiver leaves and is soothed when the parent returns. When frightened, the child will seek proximity and closeness with the parent. In other words, the securely attached child embraces, accepts, and desires closeness given by the parent. The child may accept comfort from others; however, he continues to prefer a bonded parent over all others.

A child with an **Anxious-Ambivalent** attachment style exhibits anxiety around strangers and new situations, even in the presence of the caregiver. After the caregiver departs, the child experiences extreme distress. Upon the return of the caregiver, the Anxious-Ambivalent child will exhibit reluctance and anxiety when approaching the parent. This attachment style develops due to disengaged, detached, or nonexistent parenting. In these child/parent dynamics, the child's needs have been ignored and unmet, and the child has learned that attempts at connection are inconsistently met.

A child with an **Anxious-Avoidant** attachment style exhibits behavior that tends to ignore or turn away from the caregiver. While most children will seek closeness in the face of fear or uncertainty, a child with this attachment style shows little to no interaction with his or her caregiver. Psychologists believe that this is the result of a repeatedly disengaged and emotionally detached caregiver. As a result, a child will not prefer the parent over a stranger or show distress if the parent leaves. In a sense, the Anxious-Avoidant child has resolved that their needs will not be met regardless of behavior.

Love Me, Love Me Not: Adult Attachment Styles

Research suggests that adult romantic relationships function in ways that are similar to child/caregiver relationships. For example, adults with a Secure attachment style have successful strategies to regulate their nervous system's distress signals when a partnership or relationship is stressed. Even in the absence of severe emotional upset, romantic relationships require navigating the emotional push and pull that is created in a two-person system. Their positive early experience with a caregiver pays off in the adult romantic realm.

Because they become more insecure with physical or emotional distance from a romantic partner, adults with an Anxious-Ambivalent attachment style may need to develop more robust coping skills in order to deactivate emotional upset and physiological arousal. Their early experiences with a distant caregiver, results in carrying that same emotional insecurity into their adult relationships.

A partner who is here today and gone tomorrow may register as a threat. While there may be little-to-no evidence that a business trip, for example, signals danger in a relationship, an adult with an Anxious-Avoidant attachment style may perceive distance as a potential rupture to the relationship.

OUR REPTILIAN BRAIN

In addition to learned experiences from childhood, we have evolution to thank for many of our feelings and reactions. Our instincts originate in the part of our brain referred to as the reptilian brain; the most primal and oldest section of our brain structure that helped us survive in prehistoric times. Although we are no longer living in the same world as our primitive ancestors, we still face threatening and potentially dangerous situations.

The reptilian brain is responsible for the drive to establish safety and defend territory. Danger registers on an emotional and physical level. For instance, if a vicious barking dog charges at us, our (prehistoric) reptilian brain releases a neurochemical signal to the emotional brain: *Do something now!* The limbic system releases its neurochemical signal that registers as an emotional and nervous system command: *Flight, Fight, or Freeze.*

In the case where a partner stomps-off after an argument, the threat may read emotionally as, *They don't love me anymore. I'm afraid they're leaving!* The nervous system response yells, FIGHT! Experienced as, *Oh No! Stop them from leaving!*

Individuals with an Anxious-Avoidant adult attachment style tend to get overwhelmed by the threat of perceived or actual closeness in a romantic connection. These individuals will either distance themselves before a connection can develop, or create distance by introducing obstacles and barriers to intimacy within the relationship in order to deactivate their emotional distress.

In my book, *For Love and Money*, I addressed how those who fear intimacy or closeness in relationships create distance with sexually compulsive or addictive behaviors. Physical distance can be created between individuals with alcohol, substances, or addictive work behaviors.

Emotional distance in a relationship can be as simple as shutting down intimacy in the partnership. It can also be about creating intensity outside of the union while being detached from a partner. For example, an individual may hide behind compulsive work and create intensity outside the relationship. This distraction creates plausible excuses for being absent or keeping a partner at arm's length.

EXPERIENCES IN CLOSE RELATIONSHIPS

While researchers largely agree that a person's adult attachment style is informed by their early interactions with parental attachment figures, adult relationships become increasingly complex. Children cannot choose their caregiver or change the dynamic of the attachment style of the parent. Adults, however, do have a choice of potential partner and depending on the choice, an adult attachment dynamic may change based on the styles of the two individuals involved.

One of the most popular measures of adult attachment style was developed in 1998 by researchers Brennan, Clark, and Shaver, called the "Experiences in Close Relationships Questionnaire" (ECR) later revised to the ECR-R.[6]

Both are designed to assess attachment-related anxiety and avoidance with four basic adult attachment styles (as opposed to three for infants): **Secure, Preoccupied, Fearful-Avoidant, and Dismissing-Avoidant** (See Figure 1).

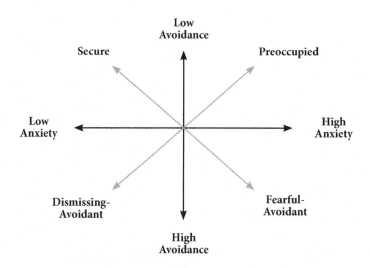

Figure 1. *The two-dimensional model of individual differences in adult attachment.*

How do the anxious and avoidant attachment patterns that form in infancy and childhood present in adult relationships? For men and women who experience adult romantic relationships as anxiety provoking, uncomfortably enmeshing, and warranting escape, early childhood bonding and attachment to caregivers was, in all likelihood, either Anxious-Ambivalent or Anxious-Avoidant. Conversely, for people who find it easy to bond, connect with, and become emotionally intimate in adult romantic relationships, early childhood bonding and attachment was usually quite secure.

Essentially, where someone finds themselves on the anxiety and avoidance axis is indicative of the extent to which that person trusts and/or fears others in adult relationships. Likewise, where a person lands on the anxiety axis determines how safe or fearful that individual feels about being in a relationship. Let's take a closer look at how each type typically behaves.

SECURE ATTACHMENT STYLE: LOW ANXIETY, LOW AVOIDANCE

• **Kate** met Lucas in college when they were each dating other people. Their paths only occasionally intersected, but when they did, they noticed how comfortable each felt in the other's presence. After graduation, they went their separate ways to pursue their careers. Kate's college relationship continued for six months beyond graduation at which time, Kate's boyfriend shared that he no longer wished to be monogamous and was interested in exploring an open sexual relationship. Kate acknowledged that he had become more distant and spent less time with her. It now made sense why he asked a month earlier to check out a swingers group under the pretense of *adding spice to our sex life*. Kate declined the offer and told him that she wanted to keep their sex life between them. When he ended their relationship soon thereafter, Kate was devastated, but she wasn't surprised.

With the help of friends, family, and therapy, Kate slowly began to rebuild her life. Even through her pain, she knew that one day she would want to be with a person who respected her. She still believed in a committed relationship and liked the emotional closeness that came with that intimacy. Kate was grieving for the early days when, as partners, each knew what mattered most to the other.

Nine months later, Kate unexpectedly ran into Lucas, an old friend from college, at a business gathering. Kate saw Lucas across the room and made her way over to where he was standing. Despite the time that had gone by, their conversation was easy and their friendship picked up almost exactly where it had left off. They caught up about their lives and eventually shared about their breakups. Along with the ease of being in each other's company, they felt a spark of attraction.

Because Kate and Lucas both possess a Secure attachment, they are able to tolerate distress while being vulnerable with others. Lucas was open about his breakup. He knew that he wasn't ready to start dating someone— even Kate—but he wanted to rekindle their connection. He was able to be vulnerable with her about how depressed he had been. Kate shared with Lucas about her struggles with depression and anxiety.

- **Courtney** began online dating after she moved for a new job. Whether or not she found a partner, she wanted to meet some people and make some new friends. Courtney identifies as bisexual, is self-assured and confident about what she has to offer. She told me she was ready for the emotional slings and arrows that online dating might provide. She confided, "I know much of this will be hit or miss; it's a numbers thing really."

Courtney is pragmatic, possesses an air of certitude, and is a natural and talented artist. After 'swiping right' on a few pictures, she decided to meet with two different women for coffee. While Courtney wasn't sure what the meetings would hold, she understood an in-person meeting was all part of the process. Before her dates she confessed, "I'm a bit nervous about meeting someone. I know my looks or personality may not hold up under in-person scrutiny." Though Courtney knew her feelings might get hurt, she weighed the risk and knew she'd be okay either way.

• **Rowan** is a financial analyst. He is also an expert climber. His status as climber is no small achievement given that Rowan was born with a congenital hand deformity, and from an early age, he struggled to overcome physical and emotional limitations. His parents were aware of how the birth defect might limit their son. They pushed him to overcome obstacles, and they worked hard to show Rowan love, encouragement, and acceptance.

Rowan was reluctant but not deterred when he began to date. He didn't see his limitations. He only saw potential. He also knew that putting himself 'out there' came with the risk of rejection from a woman who wouldn't see beyond his birth defect. Regardless, because he was raised with a Secure attachment style, he was able to summon his courage despite his insecurities and trust that his physical challenges would not deter the right partner for him.

A person with a Secure adult attachment style exhibits little to no anxiety or avoidance toward a partner. This is typically because the individual experienced secure attachment in infancy and childhood, and had a reliable caregiver who provided a safe haven and appropriate emotional co-regulation. Kate, Lucas, Courtney, and Rowan all had secure attachment dynamics with their caregiver and they are consequently able to mirror that in adult relationships.

> *A person with a Secure attachment style feels comfortable sharing power in a relationship. Such a person is not threatened by a partner's success and/or achievement and is comfortable with the focus being on the other. While other attachment styles tend to see this as disempowering or threatening, the person with a Secure attachment style rests comfortable in their own self-worth.*
>
> *Secure couples share relational power and are grounded in the notion that each brings their own unique strength to the relationship. Each recognizes that one's personal success supports the ultimate success of the relationship.*

PREOCCUPIED ATTACHMENT STYLE: HIGH ANXIETY, LOW AVOIDANCE

- **Bonnie** is compelled to check Rick's phone and laptop. Before they married, Rick shared that he had an affair years earlier. Rick has never been unfaithful in their marriage, but occasionally, when Bonnie is feeling insecure, she becomes obsessed with the fear that Rick might be cheating. She says, "I know it sounds like I'm paranoid, but I'm afraid that he'll do to me what he did before we were married. I gave up my career so that we could build his practice."

Rick has never given Bonnie any reason to worry, but her history activates her current insecurities. Bonnie's father had several affairs. As a child Bonnie witnessed her mother's anguish and often heard her mother cry late at night. It was only years later that Bonnie realized why her mother spent time at the bank trying to figure out the finances. "We made endless trips to the bank and my mother was always so anxious. I realize now that he was taking money from their savings to spend money on other women. I felt so torn about my own father; I loved him but hated how he hurt the family."

While Bonnie wants and needs Rick's affection, she is nonetheless afraid of getting too close. Rick has begun to question whether staying in the relationship is worth the struggle. He says, "I frequently reassure Bonnie that I love her, but she has a difficult time believing that I want to be with her, or that I have no desire to be with other women."

• **Alan** knows that his wife is faithful. This is the second marriage for both of them, and they care deeply about each other. Alan's first marriage ended two years earlier due to his lack of trust. At the time, Alan expressed a motivation to work on his issues regarding self-worth, but he never followed through. When Alan and his current wife were introduced by mutual friends, he tried to convince himself that he was a catch. He had to quiet his inner critical voice that said he had little to offer a partner. He marveled that such a successful woman would want him. "I know that she loves me," he says. "When we're at her work functions, I see how many other men she could have. I'm not so insecure that I think I don't deserve her, but I wonder if it is only a matter of time before she says that she is bored with me."

*   **Jane** met Ryan through mutual friends. He is a musician who has worked hard to establish his career. They met when Jane went with a group to one of his first solo performances.

Afterward, they all went out to celebrate and Jane and Ryan struck up a conversation. That night was the first of many long conversations and within a few weeks, they decided to be exclusive.

Ryan's growing popularity has become a problem for the couple. As Ryan's travel schedule becomes more demanding, Jane has asked for more assurances that Ryan actually cares about her. Perhaps due to the stress of his travel schedule, Ryan's drinking and use of marijuana has increased. To make matters worse, Jane fears that Ryan might be having affairs while on the road, and they've started to argue about Ryan possibly cutting back on his tour dates.

Jane feels increasingly invisible in the relationship and

her only recourse seems to be to control Ryan's behavior. She said, "I care about him, maybe more than he cares about himself. I know that the women who fawn over him probably don't really care about him. They just want to screw him. I'm really jealous but what can I do? My friends say that I'm trying to control him, but I'm just doing what any loving partner would do—caring about someone they love."

Consider Bonnie, Alan, and Jane. Their ever-present insecurity compromises their relationships. People with a Preoccupied attachment style become overwhelmed by their own insecurities. They may try to ease their distress with controlling behaviors, arguments, or compulsive and addictive processes to self-soothe. Many of these relationships become volatile and conflict laden.

Starting an argument or fight serves to deactivate an insecure person's vulnerability by taking charge of feeling powerless in the relationship. It may sound counterintuitive to pick a fight, but negative attention is preferable over no attention at all. This cycle is often the result of unresolved and repeated trauma from childhood.

Regardless of the ways in which a person acts out their anxiety, the result is a block to emotional closeness aimed at minimizing any potential of pain due to the end of a relationship. Other times the Preoccupied person will end the relationship altogether, thinking, "I'll hurt you before you can hurt me." However the anxiety manifests, the resulting behavior pushes the partner away from the anxious individual.

A person with a Preoccupied attachment style does not readily share or give up power in a relationship. Their power is derived from the attention and affection shown by a love interest. If that attention fluctuates, the relationship becomes fraught with emotional highs and lows. The Preoccupied person perceives the change as a signal of potential abandonment and makes frantic attempts to maintain the connection. A key motivator in relationships is to desire to avoid perceived or actual abandonment.

The power dynamics at play here are the overvaluation of another with a simultaneous devaluation of self. The driving element of this power differential is shame. Relationships with these dynamics involve a partner who exhibits shameless behavior paired with a person who sees themself as shameful, or at the least unworthy—a falsely empowered partner with a falsely disempowered one. Over time, this disparity worsens and becomes a self-defeating and vicious cycle.

FEARFUL-AVOIDANT ATTACHMENT STYLE: HIGH ANXIETY, HIGH AVOIDANCE

I first spoke about John and Judy in *For Love and Money*. Their stories are an unfortunate but accurate depiction of individuals with a Fearful-Avoidant attachment style, and are relevant in understanding how this attachment style plays into power dynamics in romantic relationships.

- **John** is a 36-year-old male who has yet to be in a romantic relationship. He is as fearful of men as he is fascinated by them, and wishes that he had the nerve to ask one out. He has worked for years in a large corporation, silently longing over several male coworkers, but never acting on his desires. Instead of approaching them and striking up a conversation, he goes home at night and lives out his fantasies in chat rooms and on porn websites.

- **Judy** spent many years in therapy hoping to heal from the wounds of childhood sexual and physical abuse. She believes most men are good, yet whenever she's approached by a man who shows an interest in her she disregards his intentions, believing that he must be as damaged as she. Furthermore, she's convinced, "if he really knew me, he would think twice about asking me out for a date."

- **David and Matt** met online and were dating for four months when Matt approached David, seeking a deeper emotional commitment. David had few significant relationships before he began to date Matt. David came to therapy because his relationship with Matt brought all of his fears to the surface. David's father abandoned the family when David was three years old. He rarely saw his father except on his birthday and Christmas. His mother was overwhelmed with being a single parent to David and his younger sister. As a child, David tried to make things better for his mother, but became overwhelmed himself. His distress in feeling unable to help, coupled with his mother's pain, left David terrified of being in relationships. He thought, "What if I'm not able to make someone happy or if what I do isn't enough? I never seem to be enough."

When Matt spoke to David about his need for more emotional intimacy, David became despondent and withdrew from the relationship. To cope, he threw himself into working long hours and binged on his favorite programs until he fell asleep. After several weeks of little to no contact, Matt came to David's house to confront him. David offered up a hollow promise that he would change, as he had done in the past, and explained his lack of action by claiming a victim mentality. He told Matt, "I'm sorry that I am such a disappointment to you."

Fearful-Avoidants dodge emotional and sexual intimacy and disengage or distance themselves in relationships due to high anxiety and high avoidance. Their attempts to deflect or otherwise avoid deep feelings can be attributed to a violent and threatening childhood family system. When we think of the word *threatening*, most people think of physical threat or harm. However, children who experience caregiving as hostile one moment and loving the next, cannot trust that their world is safe or that their caregivers will consistently protect them. This behavior pattern creates a fear of needing love and nurturing. When that fear manifests itself in adult relationships, it provokes a come-here, go-away dynamic. Typically, the approach-avoidance conflict refers to a decision or a behavior that is a simultaneously positive and negative linking of behaviors. In this case the child's desired approach behavior is seeking love and nurturing and the undesired avoidance behavior is indifference, aggression or rejection.

Because of this early double-bind, the Fearful-Avoidants cannot escape thinking about close relationships no matter how hard they try. Scientists refer to this as the ironic rebound effect whereby trying to repress thoughts tends to induce such thoughts to surface. Consequently, Fearful-Avoidants seek superficial physical/sexual encounters to supplant their thoughts of the close relationship with anonymous sex, one-night stands, online sexual encounters, pornography, and the like.

Consider John's story: In early childhood he spent many nights alone, waiting for his mother to return from her second job as a janitor, which she needed to support herself and her son. In this unfortunate way, John learned that in order to be loved and cared for, he needed to endure loneliness. In other words, he learned that love equaled abandonment.

Good Enough Parenting

John's upbringing is a painful but unintentional example of "good enough" parenting. The theory of good enough parenting supports the fact that no parenting is perfect nor are there perfect parents with boundless energy, time, and attention. In John's case, his mother did what she had to do to provide for herself and her son, but in doing so, she was unavailable to John's emotional or physical needs.

Our brains are capable of changing, and healing is always possible, even when that healing begins in therapy.

I referred earlier to my relationship with my mother. She tried her best to be attentive to her three children, but she was unable to attend to all of my needs in the way that I know I needed. With or without the three of us, I am certain that my mother was not emotionally capable or emotionally equipped to attune to me. In my adult life I've learned how to self-care and heal from those early losses, although perhaps never completely.

I am aware that my relationship with a client might be the first opportunity for them to begin healing the wounds from a breach in attachment with a caregiver. Their wounds may be the inadvertent but painful result of an absent parent or a parent overwhelmed by their life circumstances. I remind them that there is no blame. It is helpful to understand their childhood in the context in which it occurred. I tell them, it's okay to grieve for your young self. Today you can reparent yourself and be there for you in the ways that you know you need.

My eye contact and attunement to the client in therapy is vitally important. Within our therapeutic relationship, a client can finally salve the wounds of the childhood loss by feeling valued and finally being seen.

John's mother never intended to be gone, nor did she wish her son to go without as a child. As a result, in adulthood, John experiences extreme distress and shame, and becomes emotionally walled-off, preferring to remain alone rather than face the threat of what he perceives as "inevitable" abandonment.

> *A Fearful-Avoidant person uses the powers of seduction to entice a love interest, but maintains walls to protect themselves from engulfment. One who is a Fearful-Avoidant maintains power in a relationship by controlling the emotional intensity. They desire close relationships but find it difficult to be open to intimacy with others due to their fear of rejection and loss. The approach-avoid cycle is driven by fear of unlovability (high anxiety, high avoidance), similar to but different from the Dismissing-Avoidant attachment style.*

DISMISSING-AVOIDANT ATTACHMENT STYLE: HIGH AVOIDANCE, LOW ANXIETY

• **Dan** recently retired from an academic position at a large university. He was young for retirement but he was ready to move on. He said, "I'm done working with administrations that tell me what to do and how to do it." He knew that he wanted to move into his next business venture, but he also wanted to date in his limited free time. "I don't want anything serious. Anyone who wants to date me will have to understand that my commitment is to my work," he said. Dan met several women online. He told me, "I can see it now. They're all going to want something from me so I tell them up front that I'm not into anything serious. It's on them if they have a problem with the arrangement." By being upfront about his boundaries, Dan hid nothing from his dates. However, his lack of availability might have been more about his underlying Dismissing-Avoidant attachment style than his imminent work, or even his frank approach to dating.

- **Savanna** and Isaac met online and within five months, began to date each other exclusively. Now that a year has passed, Isaac has lost interest in getting together, and when Savanna reaches out via text, he responds that he is busy or unavailable. He is hesitant to make plans more than a week in advance. Desperate for advice, Savanna turned to her close girlfriends. "I can't understand why early on we were so close and he was so into us!" she cried. "Now he is distant and at times even seems to hate me. What did I do?" In an effort to engage with him, Savanna suggested that they go to couples counseling. Isaac said, "I'll go with you if that's what you really want, but I think it's a waste of our time and your money."

- **Levon** is an artist and writer and prides himself on being successful. Shortly before his 49th birthday, he began to feel depressed. This was unusual since Levon was typically upbeat and had a positive outlook on life; able to juggle several projects at the same time. To the outside world, he had everything, including success in his creative work and health. However, he felt his life was missing a deep connection with others, as well as a romantic partner.

Levon couldn't shake his depression and turned to online hook-ups in the hopes that would lift his mood. When casual sex didn't work and his depression worsened, he relented and called a therapist for help. One night while having a drink with a colleague, he confessed, "Can you believe it? This therapist told me that I'm emotionally unavailable!"

Dan, Isaac, and Levon are examples of Dismissing-Avoidant individuals. They are emotionally unavailable, and they actively disengage from real intimacy. People with a Dismissing-Avoidant attachment style often protect themselves with a wall of seduction, a manner of relating that conveys interest but does not allow for deeper emotional and relational connection. This sort of engaging behavior can be irresistibly alluring to the "neediness" of those with a Preoccupied attachment style, as their need for attention and connection is fulfilled (temporarily) by the seductive yet walled-off nature of the Dismissive-Avoidant.

Levon's lack of deep connections with others and his inability to tolerate closeness in relationships is typical of those who struggle with a Dismissing-Avoidant attachment style. It was difficult for Levon to admit that he had a problem, let alone to hear that his childhood might be the source of his depression. Therapy is a painful and difficult process and can be particularly difficult for individuals such as Levon, due to their defensive shield of inflated self-esteem and self-sufficiency—which they have created in order to suppress negative memories.

An inability to tolerate closeness stems from childhood attachments that were unavailable, critical, neglectful, or inconsistent in love and nurturing. A child who experiences too-little interaction or outright neglect, learns to be self-sufficient and counter-dependent.

> *The person with Dismissing-Avoidant attachment affirms the power position in a relationship by holding their (likely) Preoccupied partner at a distance, providing just enough attention and encouragement to keep the partner engaged. The Dismissing-Avoidant displays affection and attention followed by a wall of dismissing and distancing behaviors. This intermittent reinforcement may appear similar to the Fearful-Avoidant, but differs in that the Dismissing-Avoidant keeps emotional intimacy to a minimum or at arm's length with high avoidance and low anxiety in relationships. By appearing interested without an authentic emotional connection, the Dismissing-Avoidant can hold the more powerful position in relationships.*

As I discussed in the previous section, "good enough" parenting forms the basis for the majority of a healthy capacity for relationships. However, parenting that falls short of "good enough," or that is expressly neglectful or abusive, can create an inability for Dismissing-Avoidants to tolerate emotional intimacy in childhood and adult relationships. Adults with this attachment style will need to work hard to overcome such a painful past.

TRUE OR FALSE SELF

We began this chapter by looking at early attachment and how core relations with care caregivers significantly shape adult relationships. The attachment styles of the parent-child, serve-return only partially explains power dynamics in relationships. This exploration must also delve into our personality development and character formation.

Narcissistic parents are not willing or able to put a child's emotional needs before self. This denial of the child's emotional needs creates an environment wherein the child must ignore itself (and cease to exist psychologically), and instead attune to the adult's needs if he is to survive. Over time, a child will learn to turn off his own inner reality and instead focus on the parent's.

Levon's necessity to devalue connection (see Dismissing-Avoidant attachment above) likely began in childhood when his own parents could not or would not acknowledge his needs. Over time, he turned off his own needs for connection and developed an external mask or false self. Winnicott's work in attachment contributed the concepts of True Self, *(real self, authentic self, original self and vulnerable self)*, and False Self, *(fake self, idealized self, superficial self and pseudo self)*.

Our ego is the aspect of personality that describes our defensive, perceptual, intellectual-cognitive, and executive functions. If we are secure and have a strong self-worth, we will be able to tolerate a human experience of feeling our shame or not good enough-ness.

Conversely, if we struggle with self-worth then we will not tolerate painful emotions—specifically shame—for the greater our shame, the greater the need for a psychological disguise behind which to hide and avoid detection. Sensing we are not good enough undermines a secure sense of self.

My own years of therapy and participation in twelve-step recovery programs have helped me succeed in treating others, as well as myself, with equanimity and compassion, but I don't always succeed in reining in my arrogance and entitlement that stems from false empowerment. On most days, I am successful in this pursuit, but this is a daily practice. Being as authentic as I can in all my relationships means I am neither less nor more lovable.

In *Healing the Shame that Binds You*, John Bradshaw wrote that when we live behind a false self we can no longer be an authentic human being. To be authentic means to be spontaneous and open. Authenticity requires courage and vulnerability. When we expose our pink puppy underbelly, we allow others in, which in turn, creates a deeper, more intimate connection.

This level of intimacy can only be established by our being honest and vulnerable.

In the chapters that follow, we will delve into how shame can become an emotional mask and a false self—the foundation for narcissism and personality development. Understanding this is essential to learning to empower ourselves while not becoming a victim to financial or sexual abuse of power.

CHAPTER FOUR

Our True Selves

To be rendered powerless does not destroy your humanity. Your resilience is your humanity. The only people who lose their humanity are those who believe they have the right to render another human being powerless. They are the weak. To yield and not break that is incredible strength.

— Hannah Gadsby, *Nanette*

The human attachment process is best understood as a "we." Yet without a "you" there can be no "me," and this formation of the self is key to the exploration of power and control dynamics. We must begin with personality and character formation; the "Me" of the "We."

Personality points to who we *appear* to be, and character speaks to who we *actually* are. The definitions for personality and character are often mistakenly thought to be similar, yet they are significantly different.

Personality refers to qualities that reflect a person's characteristic patterns of thoughts, feelings, and behaviors that demonstrate (demonstrate being the operative word here) consistency and stability over time. In essence, personality represents what others observe in our outer selves.

Character refers to the inner self—the internal, distinguishing, mental, and moral characteristics of a person. Together character and personality make up the separate and unique self.

SELECTION PERCEPTION: HALOS AND HORNS

Psychological studies have shown that humans have a natural bias toward attractiveness over unattractiveness. We will also extend positive character traits to people we perceive as attractive without knowing the accuracy of this assessment. Think of an attractive person you have seen at work or in social settings but have yet to meet. Likely, your positive cognitive bias will influence you to perceive that person as potentially more intelligent, outgoing, confident, or trustworthy than in reality. "Wow," you might say to yourself. "I want to meet that person."

Similarity, our first impressions of a date or potential partner may or may not prove to be accurate. We tend to believe that *what* we observe about someone (personality) is the same as who that someone is (character). This tendency to perceive information about those we are attracted to is a phenomenon American psychologist Edward Thorndike called the Halo Effect.

In an experiment, Thorndike asked commanding officers in the military to evaluate a variety of qualities in their subordinate soldiers such as leadership, physical appearance, intelligence, loyalty, and dependability. The experiment revealed a human error in reasoning in which we form a favorable impression from a single trait or characteristic. For example, a tall and attractive sub-ordinate was perceived as being the most intelligent and ranked overall as "better" than his peers. Thorndike found that physical appearances are the most influential in determining our overall impressions of other peoples' character.

In 1946, Solomon Asch, a Polish-born psychologist and pioneer in social psychology, elaborated on Thorndike's research. He found that individuals formed lasting impressions of one another based on premature or initial information, lending potency to the adage you only get one chance to make a good first impression. Nowhere is this more evident than on dating sites.

FIRST IMPRESSIONS

In the dating and mating world, when we meet that special someone and our first impression of them is very positive, the Halo Effect kicks into full gear. We might ignore the negative characteristics and concentrate only on the positive ones. Similarly, Thorndike's research revealed the Horn Effect which names the cognitive bias in which we tend to ignore any evidence of positive behaviors or personality traits, concentrating instead on the negative. A negative first impression predicts a higher probability that we will not like a person based on an initial negative experience.

So, how can we really know what a person's true character is? Can we bypass assumptions and simply apply a "What You See Is What You Get" logical approach to life? Not if we want to be realistic. Humans are complicated. In addition to the biases we each have, we can be counted on to shapeshift and engage defensive masks and false selves as protective measures. We each have a shadow side, a suppressed, repressed, or rejected self that represents internalized guilt, shame, or other painful trauma.

When a couple arrives for their initial session in therapy, I ask how they first met. This query serves multiple purposes. First, it's a natural way to determine the couple's emotional connection (despite the stressors that brought them into therapy), and I can observe the way in which the partners communicate about one another while sharing mutual information. Second, it is an organic way to gather vital information about the couple's history.

Frequently couples describe to me an early meeting that resulted in one partner disliking the other based on what he or she said or did. Notice how much information is revealed in the following anecdote:

When we first met I was so nervous and awkward! I opened the door to the restaurant and walked in first and left Shelley outside to fend for herself. This would have never happened if I weren't so nervous and trying NOT to do something stupid! I had to work hard to come back from total rejection. She wasn't having it or me for several months! Finally, she agreed to go on a second date with me.

LIMERENCE

It takes time and consistency to truly know someone. Most of us put our best foot forward when we meet others, particularly when a potential love interest may be involved. In the early stage of romantic attraction in a relationship, we experience limerence, a natural and involuntary state of sexual and emotional infatuation and obsessional thinking about the other person. During this phase, we instinctively emphasize our best qualities and characteristics to enhance our chances of acceptance and avoid rejection by the object of our obsession. At the same time, the positive cognitive bias influences us to judge that other person as (potentially) more intelligent, outgoing, confident, or trustworthy than they may be in reality.

This stage can last anywhere between one and three years, on average. With time, each individual's true personality and character reveals itself. In the initial stage of limerence, the relationship will either grow into an affectional or sexual love, or it will fade.

It is important to note that the limerent phase of attraction is particularly addictive for those with the Preoccupied and Dismissing-Avoidant attachment styles. A Preoccupied has a strong need for love, acceptance, and reassurance, all of which are activated by the potential love interest's adoration and attention. This can also be self-activated with fantasy and obsessional thinking about the partner. The Dismissing-Avoidant will initially employ charm and seduction to seduce, and is hooked by the conquest and allure of the love interest. Ultimately, once the conquest is actualized, the Dismissing-Avoidant will often lose interest, as this level of intensity becomes too "demanding" of time and attention—because there isn't the intention or ability for emotional vulnerability, or because there isn't a love interest. As a result, the Dismissing-Avoidant withdraws their attention. This intensifies the Preoccupied's underlying fear of abandonment and longing for emotional or sexual closeness.

Problems arise when we jump to conclusions, acting on our first impressions, believing something to be true based solely on what we see. The ways in which we process information or use mental shortcuts to appraise others is often filtered through the lens of our attachment style and experiences with significant others in childhood. Our desire to trust others early in a relationship may be a glass-half-full approach to life, but consistent interaction with a person offers the best gauge of his or her personality and character across time and place. This happens after the powerful draw of the initial limerence phase has subsided. Consider Isaac whom we met in Chapter Three, the Dismissing-Avoidant. Savanna and Isaac's relationship had matured beyond the limerence phase and exposed the underlying entitlement of Isaac's true self.

Isaac was unsympathetic to Savanna's attempts to connect with him. She couldn't understand why Isaac had been so attentive early on but now seemed disinterested. When Savanna suggested that they go to therapy, he dismissed her effort to work on their relationship. Although Isaac agreed to her request for therapy, notice there was no emotional or financial investment since he indicated he wouldn't pay for therapy since he saw the process as a waste of his time and "her" money.

From a relationship perspective, Isaac's response did little to build any emotional connection and Savanna might be wise to consider this when deciding whether or not to move forward in their relationship. Diving deeper into Isaac's family of origin and childhood, we can better understand his response and how he views relationships. Let's take a look.

KING BABY

Isaac was born for greatness. His parents hoped their third and last child would be a boy. Isaac Jr. didn't disappoint. His older sisters coddled him and his parents held high hopes for him. Isaac's mother referred to him as her "prince." There was little if anything that Isaac could do wrong. When Isaac was young his father traveled often for business, but when he was home the two spent time together working on computers. It didn't matter that eight-year-old Isaac didn't understand computers or that he preferred instead to play with his cars while his father tinkered. Isaac really wanted his father to play catch, but they were together and as Isaac's father said, "We are doing important work." To his father, that was all that mattered.

Discipline in the family fell to Isaac's mother and older sisters. His mother's "no" often meant "yes," and Isaac learned that he could talk his way out of any small problem at home by lying or bending the truth. Batting his piercing blue-gray eyes, he could wiggle his way into or out of situations at will.

By the time Isaac was thirteen years old, he preferred sports over studying. His grades were passing but not stellar. He learned to get by and maintain an average grade in school with enough effort to stay out of detection and off his parents' radar. Isaac avoided his mother's requests about his grades and fended her off by lying about how well he was doing. He boasted about being one of the smartest kids in his class, which delighted his mother and father. A simple lie was all it took for Isaac to appease his parents' bothersome demands about his grades and schoolwork.

Isaac could have excelled academically had he tried, but he didn't have to. Neither parent held him accountable. His father gloated about his sporting agility as if it was his own, and his mother rarely enforced any restrictions on studying before social activities. His parents' blind adulation taught Isaac that the world still revolved around him. He was stuck in King Baby Syndrome (the female equivalent of which is Queen Baby), a term first coined by Tom Cunningham at the Hazelden Foundation in Minnesota. Those with King Baby Syndrome have not outgrown the early stages of self-centered gratification—innate to infancy and young childhood—with appropriate levels of self-esteem and mutuality toward others.

When parents do not allow children to fail or express their true self, the child is forced into a psychological double-bind: either please the parent and betray their own true self, or risk abandonment and rejection by the parent when the child asserts their own needs and wants.

Fear of abandonment and rejection by a parent may be real or imagined. Infants are entirely dependent upon the love and support of a caregiver, and will avoid a threat or disconnection to a primary attachment. The psychological distress of perceived or real abandonment by a primary caregiver remains one of the strongest causes of human distress and dysfunction. When we experience a threat to this connection, it triggers a fear response referred to as separation stress or separation anxiety. This anxiety might be masked by arrogance, rage, or both.

Isaac's parents needed him to appear successful and enabled his perpetual state of emotional immaturity and self-centeredness. Isaac's parents forced greatness upon him at birth and created his false self, an exaggerated sense of entitlement, self-obsession, self-importance, and grandiosity.

Beneath the veneer of Isaac's uniqueness lay a worrisome academic performance and lack of accountability. More troublesome was the family's counterattack against the school when they attempted to hold Isaac accountable to academic rigor. As his family saw it, the school made Isaac a scapegoat. They (falsely) alleged that teachers singled out and targeted Isaac due to his criticism of the school's alcohol policy as overly restrictive toward athletes. "The school is retaliating for our son's outspoken and valiant behavior!" they protested. Refusing to admit he might be at fault, they defended their son in spite of evidence to the contrary and instead of holding him accountable they were outraged at any perceived offense.

Isaac's parents continued to make allowances and excuses for him throughout his life. The person they had created was now becoming an imposter. Outwardly, Isaac exuded arrogance and an overconfident air of success. He declared himself the most popular among his peers and proclaimed that he was heading for greatness. Inwardly, Isaac was unsure of who he was and hid his deepening insecurity and mounting defensive rage. Most of all, King Baby was afraid that others would discover the truth only he knew: that he was a failure. The "prince," now a King, felt like a fraud.

Now that we know Isaac's story, his response to Savanna's request to attend therapy, while unfortunate, makes sense. Isaac's false-self shielded deep insecurities at the core of his fragile ego and narcissistic wounds.

Take a moment to read the list of King Baby characteristics commonly associated with entitlement. These traits will help you identify the presence of a false self and any potential warning signs of problematic power and control dynamics in relationships:

KING BABY CHARACTERISTICS

- They make good first impressions

- Express entitlement

- They people-please, seeking approval from others

- Have difficulty accepting criticism

- Hypersensitive to feedback

- Have addictive personality

- Believe that normal rules do not apply to them

- Are easily provoked to anger and rage

- Given to exaggeration and showing off

- Appear grandiose when surrounded by people

- Rarely take responsibility

- Rarely admit to wrongdoing

- Complain and blame others for their own wrongdoing

- Believe that they are entitled to people, places, and things

- Fear failure and rejection

- Boast about sexual conquest, money, and material objects

- Display a lack of real emotion

King Babies are like the hunter Narcissus of Greek mythology. His mother was warned in a prophecy that her beautiful son would live a long life if he never saw his reflection. When he finally saw his own beguiling image in the water, he was entranced and fell in love with that illusion of a person. He refused to leave the water's edge. Resourceful as he was, his obsession with that false person caused his death.

The myth of Narcissus foreshadows Isaac's real life story. It's possible for Isaac to prevent his own demise, but he must be willing to accept some realities and heed caution. However, Isaac is not interested in change. His self-absorption can only terminate in his tragic fall from greatness, resulting in his ignoble psychological death.

This is the irony of narcissism, which we explore in depth in the next chapter.

CHAPTER FIVE

NARCISSISM AND THE
WINDS OF SHAME

*O fondly foolish boy, why vainly seek to clasp
a fleeting image? What you seek is nowhere;
but turn yourself away, and the object of your
love will be no more. That which you behold is
but the shadow of a reflected form and has no
substance of its own. With you it comes, with you
it stays, and it will go with you—if you can go.*

— Ovid, *Metamorphoses*

Few words elicit as strong a reaction as narcissism. We reduce others with the accusation that they're being "narcissistic" if they act self-absorbed or self-centered. We worship the escapades of the rich and famous, internet sensations, and social influencers, but we just as quickly denounce their behavior as narcissistic and self-serving. When we watch these same celebrities fall, we feel a sense of schadenfreude. It's a complex brew.

Long before our modern-day fascination with narcissists, the mythical Kronos ruled supreme in the Golden Age after having defeated his father. His myopic delusion of grandiosity led him to think that he was safe from his own political demise prophesied by his parents.

Kronos was unwilling to consider that he was vulnerable. He overestimated his own attributes while underestimating others. In his arrogance, ultimately, he was bested by his own child, Zeus.

The Greek myth of Daedalus and Icarus is another cautionary tale against arrogance. In order to escape the island of Crete where the two were imprisoned, Daedalus constructed wings made of wax. Icarus dismissed his father's caution to not fly too close to the sun for fear the wax might be melted by the sun's heat. Icarus believed that he was impervious to demise, but soon tumbled out of the sky and fell into the sea, as predicted, where he drowned.

Icarus, Kronos and Narcissus all share a single-minded solipsism and all fell from their mutual tragic flaw: excessive pride.

Self-esteem Across the Spectrum

Narcissism was introduced as a psychological concept in 1914 by Sigmund Freud and was formally introduced as a personality disorder and character in 1925 by Freud's colleague, Robert Waelder.

The term "narcissistic personality structure" came into use in the late 60s and was popularized in TV and movies. The term Narcissistic Personality Disorder was introduced in 1980 into the American Psychiatric Association's reference, *Diagnostic and Statistical Manual of Mental Disorders, Third Edition (DSM-III)*. The current *DSM-V* refers to NPD as a pervasive pattern of grandiosity, an unfulfilled need for admiration, and a lack of empathy.[1]

The term "narcissistic" is commonly used to describe a person who is mildly self-centered or self-absorbed. Depending on a situation or life circumstance, this behavior can be quite normal. However, Narcissistic Personality Disorder (NPD) presents across a wide range of functioning, often exposing a fragile sense of self. People with this disorder consistently demonstrate a lack of empathy and, in fact, studies show that people with NPD often have less brain matter in areas related to empathy.

Researchers in Germany conducted an imaging study of the brains of individuals who suffer from NPD. The study showed that their brains are indeed abnormal—they have less gray matter in a part of the cerebral cortex called the left anterior insula.

The structural abnormalities in this region have been linked to empathy or deficits in empathic resonance. The researchers also found that the left anterior insula—a region of the brain involved with cognitive functioning and regulation of emotion—is potentially tied to the expression of compassion and empathy. While it is as yet unclear how these brain abnormalities develop, researchers have the evidence to show that brain structure contributes to the narcissist's absence of empathy.

However, there are fundamental differences between individuals who lack empathy for their victims and fearlessly exploit the vulnerable, and individuals who lack empathy or lean into fearlessness—perhaps even learn to ignore fear altogether, but would not be diagnosed as a psychopath.[2]

Consider a spectrum of self-esteem. On one end of this spectrum is healthy, non-pathological self-love, healthy in that such esteem allows us to assert our needs and wants in the world. On the other end of the spectrum is pathological narcissism. Individuals at this end show no regard or consideration for others. Working with or being in a relationship with people who have above average narcissistic traits may pose challenges, but differs from being in a relationship with a person who has NPD.

So what exactly *is* narcissism?

- A perpetual yearning or longing to be of sole importance to another human being that drives the personality structure
- A mask that grows out of a disconnection from the authentic self
- Dependency enshrouded by grandiosity
- A compensation for the shame and insufficiency of self

Narcissists are drawn to power. Their inflated self-perception feeds their rise through leadership ranks, and fuels a need for greater amounts of admiration and adulation. The grandiosity creates a vicious feedback loop and a predilection for unethical behavior. A narcissistic personality often lacks empathy necessary for close and intimate relationships. On the furthest end of the spectrum are the pathological and malevolent behaviors belonging to The Dark Triad: Narcissism, Machiavellianism, and psychopathy—three interrelated but conceptually distinct personality constructs.[3]

I previously wrote about narcissism in *For Love and Money,* in Chapter Seven.

My years of experience on Wall Street introduced me to a wealth of men who engaged in impression management, self-centered, and power grabbing behaviors. Some behaviors were merely arrogant and some were outright sociopathic. Greater numbers of women eventually climbed their way to loftier bastions of power but that wasn't until a decade or so later. In the go-go years of the '80s and '90s, investment banks were brimming with throngs of young, gluttonous traders and bankers riding the crest of financial excess and glory. The stories of men who enjoyed a meteoric rise to professional and personal heights, only to then plunge into a financial and personal crash and burn were legendary.

Some men saw their "fall from grace" as a painful summons to a deeper, more introspective place, yet many more continued to addictively pursue the never-ending cycle of self-destructive behaviors – financial shenanigans, moral superiority, and sexual excess – while remaining oblivious to the inevitable, refusing to believe their shameless monetary and sexual escalation would once again inevitably lead to collapse. As they repeated this self-destructive downward spiral, one could only postulate what fueled their never-ending pursuit of all things narcissistic.

People with deeper narcissistic ego wounds live with a gaping insufficiency of self. They are driven entirely by their obsessional focus on conquest, achievement, and adulation. American psychologist Henry A. Murray published his Icarus Complex theory in 1955, suggesting that human behavior is driven by an internal state of disequilibrium. "We have a LACK of something and this drives us. We are dissatisfied and we desire something"[4]

Narcissistic Supply

In a previous chapter, we met Isaac. His parents made allowances and excuses for their son. Their untiring exaltation sustained their own delusions about his greatness and enabled Isaac's entitled self to flourish into a diagnosable narcissistic personality disorder. This is an example of narcissistic supply, a term that refers to people, places, and/or things that provide the narcissist a constant source of attention, approval, adoration, and admiration—the proverbial food that feeds the beast.

Being loved by someone else solves the problem of having failed to live up to one's own ideal self. Conversely, having a supply of people or things upon which to focus adoration fills the void. Examples of narcissistic supply may include others—partners, children, co-workers, but also rage, dysphoria, boredom, depression, and/or anxiety.

Therapists can rank high on a narcissist's list as someone they need to impress, or, from whom they seek approval. For this reason, a client who has a strong narcissistic ego wound, and uses therapy to impress rather than as an opportunity to grow, will achieve little to no growth in therapy. The narcissist's fragile ego does not allow for introspective reflection. That fragile layer remains protected from exposure by others, much less the introspective process of therapy. Like Narcissus who could not bear to disrupt his own image by touching the water's surface, a narcissist cannot tolerate the distress and disillusioning induced by introspection in therapy.

BEN

Years ago, I worked in an inpatient treatment facility where Ben was a patient. I had seen Ben for three sessions. From the beginning, he held to the belief that he had little to do with his current circumstances: he had just been fired and his wife was threatening to leave him unless he got help. He denied any responsibility.

In our fourth session, I challenged him in this assertion. I hoped that Ben could tolerate this level of emotional tension.

I was wrong.

Ben unleashed a defensive sound-wall of excuses and deflections and at the same time, he let me know that he doubted my skills as a therapist. To ward off a hint of "lack," a fragile ego must have an external source for literal or figurative survival. The narcissist performs a self-deluded hat trick to manipulate and control the supply source around him or, in this case, to eliminate the threat—the therapist. This is a fragile ego's survival tactic.

A narcissist believes they are needless, wantless, and beyond depending on others. This is clearly a delusion. To be human is to be interdependent and in need of others. Specifically, if Ben had not needed my approval, he might have been better able to tolerate my questioning of his version of events. A narcissist's seeming independence masks a very deep dependence on their "supply." The supply source must remain under their control and in service to their needs. Any deviation from this position will elicit a rageful attack on the transgressor; any supply is better than no supply at all, if they fear they are about to lose something.

I recognized that Ben had far to go but I hoped that he could put down his armor long enough to look behind his fragile mask. For any therapist, knowing how far to push against a narcissistic defense is an art, not a science. I learned a lesson that day, and I remain ever-vigilant and aware; honor the wound and tread lightly.

Despite a narcissist's best attempts to manipulate life itself, it is inevitable that loss will occur. For instance, a narcissist's partner may reject his sexual advances, he may be terminated from a job, or receive a letter of rejection from a respected high-status figure. In that case, the narcissist will experience:

- A regressed self
- Overt and/or covert rage as a defense mechanism
- Shame core revealed
- Desperate search for alternative sources in people or objects of desire
- Desperate attempts to re-engage the supply
- Depression and/or anxiety
- Self-medicating and/or addictions (drugs, alcohol, sex, money, or work)

DAVE'S STORY

Dave was bored with his current job and decided that it was time to leave that position for a more exciting business venture. Before he took that leap he wanted to date. He said, "I don't want anything serious. Anyone who wants to date me will have to understand that my primary commitment is to my work."

Let's take a closer look at Dave.

Dave was married for five years. He was quick to share with anyone who would listen that his marriage ended because of his wife's lack of affection and her drinking. His colleagues had not met his former wife—they had divorced before he joined the company—but his stories elicited their empathy and compassion. By garnering their sympathy, Dave believed his peers would see him as successful.

Dave's an all-in kind of guy. He commits to his professional endeavors and pours his energy into every project. Dave can also be grandiose and flaunt an air of self-importance, but his colleagues and friends excuse the behavior, crediting Dave's strong personality and his desire for everyone to excel. "Dave is demanding of those around him," they say, "but he is equally demanding of himself."

Rumors circulate that Dave may be dating or perhaps he's in a relationship, but being notoriously private, nothing can be confirmed. When asked if he would like to bring a date to a company event, Dave declines, adding, "We prefer to spend time alone when we both get the chance."

With these traits, Dave could be considered Dismissing-Avoidant. These individuals create distance in a relationship and are reluctant to allow a deep connection with others. They are two feet out before they ever put one foot in. In addition, Dave's behavior—grandiosity, and self-importance—are indicative of a mask protecting a fragile personality, concealing emotionally abusive behavior and hidden manipulation.

Dave also meets criteria for NPD.

In relationships, Dave fixates on his partner's character and self-esteem. He highlights *her* faults. If she has a healthy level of self-esteem, she will see that the relationship is ill fated, and exit before Dave's emotional and psychological abuse create a lasting negative impact.

Dave's narcissistic tactics create confusion for his partners. Depending on the severity of their childhood attachment wounds, narcissists like Dave learn to shut off feeling guilt or remorse and will be unable to exhibit empathy at the loss of the relationship. If the wounds are severe and lean toward the pathological end of the spectrum, they may even enjoy the sadistic reward of hurting another person.

A narcissist is dependent upon people, places, and things for purpose and self-worth. Without the benefit of someone or something supplying that sense of purpose and self-worth, the narcissist's Achilles heel of buried shame is exposed. They will employ fantasy (self-medicating or addictive behaviors) or escape to restrain the flood of self-loathing and potential suicidal ideation.

SHAME DYNAMICS IN RELATIONSHIP

"To be shame-bound means that whenever you feel any feeling, need or drive, you immediately feel ashamed. The dynamic core of your human life is grounded in your feelings, needs and drives. When these are bound by shame, you are shamed to the core," writes John Bradshaw in *Healing the Shame that Binds You.*

In unhealthy relationships, an insecure partner may take on the narcissist's projected shamelessness as their own identity. The narcissist's covert shame becomes the partner's overt shame—their "cross to bear." Holding a narcissist's shame in lieu of holding a narcissist accountable is, unfortunately, common. It's what happens with many disempowered partners. Over the years, I have found that individuals who grew up in shame-based and rigid family systems share a predisposition toward holding the shame. Unconsciously, they relegate themselves to the "Shame FULL" and "One Down" position in a relationship, as seen in Figure 2 below. This compensatory act both consciously and unconsciously manifests an internal sense of unworthiness predating the relationship and stemming from childhood. The source of the shame is the same for the narcissist as it is for the partner—a shame core.

Figure 2. *Adapted from Pia Mellody's Post Induction Training*

Though unpleasant, for the partner in the Shame FULL and One Down position, this is an old and familiar default, and therefore, it feels preferable. The One Down position is a more life-preserving stance, since it does not require confrontation. In essence, to confront the narcissist would also force their partners to confront their own sense of shame, anger, pain, fear, and self-doubt about ever being "good enough." From this One Down position a partner has learned to comfortably dwell in the "land of the shameful."

Although a narcissist's Shame LESS and One Up position also stems from, and is driven by a shame core, the narcissist manifests his or her low self-worth with a counteractive stance of "better than." This self-entitled narcissistic facade is a compensatory, albeit thinly veiled offensive measure against a fragile ego and fear about being "not good enough." Ultimately, it bolsters rather than diminishes one's internal feeling of "less than," despite the outwardly projected mastery of self. The greater the insecurities of the individual are, the greater the defense and potential for pathological displays.

TOWARD THE DARKER END OF THE SPECTRUM

As fascinating as narcissism is, this disordered thinking occupies but one corner of a pathological extreme known as The Dark Triad. The three interrelated but conceptually distinct personality traits in the Dark Triad are narcissism, Machiavellianism, and psychopathy.

Fewer explorations on psychology garner as much curiosity, or perhaps, deserve as much elaboration than this triad. While some personality traits are colorful or subversive, The Dark Triad defy socially sanctioned or accepted practices. At best, the outcomes can be unnerving. At worst, the outcomes are ruinous, or even life threatening.

Exploring The Dark Triad and the darker side of relationships may not be for the faint of heart; however, it is fundamental to an exploration on power dynamics, certainly where sex or money are involved, and so that is where we begin our next chapter.

CHAPTER SIX

THE DARK SIDE OF POWER

*Psychopaths, rather than having an
impairment in recognizing the emotions
of others, indeed have a talent for it.
And that the problem lies not in emotional
recognition per se, but in the dissociation
between its sensory and affective components:
in the disconnect between knowing what
an emotion is and feeling what it's like.*

— Kevin Dutton

A t one time or another almost all individuals in a relationship feel harmed or inadvertently hurt by the other person. Pain in a relationship is unavoidable, but a very troubling—and potentially dangerous—power dynamic results when a person consciously inflicts harm on the other, or worse, derives satisfaction from doing so. This signals a much darker power differential and veers toward the pathological manifestation of personality. In the exploration of power and control it is essential to identify extreme manifestations of exploitation and its associated personality traits to prevent manipulation in your own relationship.

TITANS AND TYRANTS

In Greek myth, power and control are synonymous with sexuality and sexual violence. In tales of incest, murder, and sexual exploitation we see fear and sexual conquest as elemental to power constructs.

As we read in an earlier chapter, the youngest of the Titan offspring, Kronos, deposed his father, Uranus by castrating him in an ambush. This ultimate emasculation began Kronos' systematic reign of pathological exploitation. He later married his sister, Rhea, and sired twelve offspring. In fear of a prophecy foretelling Kronos' own overthrow, he swallowed each of his children as they were born; however, Rhea saved their youngest, Zeus, by hiding him away on the island of Crete.

When Zeus grew up, he forced his father to disgorge his siblings and led them in an uprising against the Titans in power. The resulting ten-year battle was called the Titanomachy. The twelve triumphant sibling gods created a majestic home on Mount Olympus and became known as The Olympians. According to the myth, at the end of the war Zeus took his father Kronos' sickle, formerly used to castrate Uranus, and cut Kronos into pieces. Zeus became the king of the gods. Although Zeus denounced human decadence and sacrifice, his own misconduct was no less depraved.

Zeus, God of sky and thunder, ruled from top of Mount Olympus. He was supreme leader and was venerated by his fellow Olympians. Although Zeus denounced human decadence and sacrifice and used violence to terrorize humans, he was not beyond his own Olympian misdeeds.

According to Greek myth, his sexual rampage began with his raping his sister, Demeter, and then later was responsible for kidnapping and raping his daughter, Persephone, who was born out of his assault on Demeter. He raped and sexually assaulted the nymph, Callisto, and Leda in the likeness of a swan. Zeus' brother, Poseidon, who lost his battle to Zeus for supreme leader and settled instead for lord of the sea, had a temper and punished those who betrayed him. In some versions of Greek myth, he raped Medusa, who thereafter was turned into a monster.

Breaking the Cycle

From the first Greek gods and goddesses, to the rise of the Titans, and later to their overthrow by the Olympians, succession cycles are a natural dynamic among the gods. Obtaining and maintaining power required craft, compromise, and violent brute force. Kronos castrated Uranus—both literally in the context of the story, as well as figuratively in terms of his power over the gods and his ability to act as ruler and father.

The need to extricate myself out from under my father's enmeshment required that I remove him from power with an equally abrupt but no less brutal action—a metaphorical Greek castration on par with Kronos'. In my case—and in the case of others who are enmeshed with parents—this meant an emotional castration of our relationship necessary for me to establish healthy boundaries in my own romantic relationships, and later, in my marriage.

Emotional and physical distance were key to allowing my independence and self-empowerment to flourish, but I was not prepared for what surfaced: rage. My rage came from years of being emotionally and sexually enmeshed and disempowered, and it fueled years of sexual aggression, a compensation for my disempowered self. At times my rage felt violent, but I never expressed it that way. It did, however, feel satisfyingly vengeful.

THE DARK SIDE

Evocative of Greek mythology, two modern-day Olympians held dominion from their mounts. In 2020, Harvey Weinstein, famous movie mogul and producer, added a new title to his long list of credits: sex offender. After years of heavy-handed threats and sizable payments to silence his female accusers, Weinstein was successfully charged with multiple counts of sexual assault and rape. He was convicted in 2020. Weinstein's power was in his authoritarian Midas grip within his industry.

Similarly, the late Jeffrey Epstein was a business financier with ties to wealth and high-profile social circles. Epstein was also a convicted sex offender—a fact many who solicited him for money and social entrée knew, but chose to ignore. Epstein's power was his financial wealth and access promised to solicitors in exchange for his unimpeded sexual access to poach and rape young girls. His death by asphyxiation in a New York City jail in late 2019 was ruled a suicide.

Like Zeus and Poseidon, these two modern day Olympians were feared more than venerated by their human victims.

The lurid details of the sexual and financial domination by Weinstein and Epstein have been widely documented. Both men bear characteristic associations with The Dark Triad, a psychological construct that refers to three personality traits: narcissism, Machiavellianism, and psychopathy. People with these traits use sexual and financial rage as weapons for power and control. By studying these key factors, you, the reader, will be able to safely assess sexual and financial abuse in a relationship.

THREE DARK TRAITS

In psychology, the Dark Triad refers to three associated and interrelated personality traits: narcissism, Machiavellianism, and psychopathy. They are called "dark" because of their malevolent qualities.

Narcissism is the first personality trait in the triad. As we have explored in a previous chapter, narcissism is excessive self-centeredness that disallows empathy and thrives on the "supply" of others' adulation, praise, or emotions. Those with this malady believe they deserve admiration and special treatment.

Machiavellianism is a personality trait referring to a person who will manipulate others to reach their own goals. They'll deceive and exploit in the interest of personal gain. The name is derived from the sixteenth century Italian politician and diplomat-turned-author, Niccolo Machiavelli.

Psychopathy, perhaps the most dangerous of the three interrelated traits, is characterized by antisocial behavior, impulsivity, selfishness, and callous disregard for others.

The three are distinct traits yet share overlapping characteristics such as a lack of empathy and interpersonal hostility.

Weinstein and Epstein likely have personalities in The Dark Triad. Our fascination with them may be in part due to a sense of disbelief. While the majority of us would crumble under the weight of fear, repulsion, or guilt, those at the darkest end of the personality spectrum—like Weinstein and Epstein—operate with cold reptilian precision. Do individuals who score high in this malevolent personality cluster of narcissism, Machiavellianism, and psychopathy lack a moral compass or not have one at all? Let's explore that here.

TRAIT THEORY

In psychology, trait theory is an approach to the study of habitual patterns of human behavior, thought, and emotions. Early pioneers in the field suggested a model to classify aspects of personality referred to as the Big Five personality trait model. It consists of five identified traits:

- Extraversion (or Extroversion)
- Agreeableness
- Openness
- Conscientiousness
- Neuroticism

Kevin Dutton is a British psychologist and author of the book, *The Wisdom of Psychopaths: What Saints, Spies, and Serial Killers Can Teach Us About Success.*[1] Dutton researches the spectrum of psychopathy and what he refers to as its positive and negative sides. His research indicates that individuals who meet diagnostic criteria for psychopathy are part of a specific subgroup of the population who possess, to varying degrees, a distinct set of personality characteristics:

- Ruthlessness
- Fearlessness
- Impulsivity
- Self-confidence
- Focus
- Coolness under pressure

Studies at the University of Texas found, "psychopathy is related to parasitic behavior that is both antisocial and high-risk. Such individuals are unlikely to consider consequences when engaging in selfish financial behavior, even in the face of punishment and financial loss."[2]

The psychopath's parasitic behavior is similar to a narcissist's supply; both seek to exploit people, places, and things as "supply" to compensate for their underdeveloped identity and insufficiency of self.

Are these the same people who reject prosocial acts of kindness, exhibit fearlessness, or show a lack of empathy toward those that are in pain? The answer is, well, yes *and* no. There are other reasons why people might exhibit some, but not all, of those features.

According to Dutton, a diagnosis of psychopathy is ultimately determined by several criteria, such as where one resides on the personality spectrum, the extent to which these personality characteristics manifest, and how they mix, combine, and deploy in a specific context. In other words, to one degree or another, a psychopath exists in all of us.

CALM UNDER PRESSURE

When I was on Wall Street, I traded commodity options. Without exception, that career required a high degree of emotional grit to navigate the financial swings in the markets. Consequently, I learned to exhibit a fair degree of fearlessness, self-confidence, focus, and coolness under pressure—four of Dutton's six distinct personality characteristics of a psychopath. Does this make me a psychopath or just a cool cucumber? Possessing some degree of each of the traits don't equal psychopathy.

Not long ago, I was near the end of a hike when, in the middle of the path, I unexpectedly came upon a mountain lion, just ten short feet away. Sightings of wildlife are common where I live, but I have never once encountered a bobcat, much less a mountain lion. On this day, a beautiful, yet potentially dangerous creature stood staring directly at me, standing directly between me and my home.

Why wasn't she moving? Was she protecting something, like a fresh kill? Maybe I shouldn't look her in the eyes, but rather, glance away as when confronted by an aggressive or scared dog. I should have been scared, but I wasn't. Rather, I was fascinated. The mountain lion owned the path and I wasn't going to cross her plain, even if I had to wait it out because she stood between my home and me. I fixed on her gaze. Just as I wondered how long this unwavering standoff might continue, her eyes shifted imperceptibly at something that stirred. Before I could look, not one, but two mountain lion cubs leapt from a tree above. Just as quickly as they landed, they scampered off with their protective mother at their back. It was thrilling.

Because I had battled the force of my father's will in my youth, I had honed my ability to remain calm and collected in times of crisis. These earlier life experiences conditioned me for power struggles with apex predators on Wall Street. So too, they had prepared me for that moment on the path.

For me, both as a financial option trader and therapist, research on a financial risk taker or narcissistic individual is not just intriguing; it's invaluable to differentiating power dynamics wherein psychopathy is involved. In those situations, therapeutic intervention is unlikely to result in substantial change. A quick and safe exit from the relationship is the best option.

A point I made earlier cannot be overstated: identifying extreme manifestations of exploitation and its associated personality traits is critical. It's the only way to prevent manipulation in your own relationship.

Let us zipline away from The Dark Triad to explore less extreme manifestations of power and control that involve sexual and financial exploitation. We start with Elsa's story.

ELSA

"Hello?"

The voice startled me. I had left the front door of my office open to allow in some fresh air. I turned and saw a well-dressed, petite woman standing in the doorway. She had a bright smile, cheerful eyes, and appeared to be in her sixties.

"I'm sorry to surprise you. I'm Elsa."

Three weeks earlier, Elsa had called to schedule an appointment. During our initial call Elsa sounded hesitant—or perhaps even embarrassed—to schedule a session. She said, "I'm calling to make an appointment. Well, actually, I wondered if you might be you taking new patients..." The rising pitch at the end of her statement transformed it into a question. This common vocal speech pattern, referred to as "uptalk," is often a cultural tendency or, as I believed for Elsa, a demonstration of doubt and uncertainty.

Once I recovered from my surprise, I welcomed Elsa in. She settled on the far side of the couch. She avoided my gaze, instead surveying the built-in bookshelves until something caught her eye. She leaned over and squinted. "I love your Sigmund Freud action figure," she said. "That's hysterical!"

I smiled. I'd forgotten Sigmund was there. "I have to admit, I love the irony." We chuckled together.

"I wonder what Sigmund would say if he knew," Elsa said.

Elsa grew silent and began to nervously fidget. She needed some help collecting her thoughts so I prompted her. "Let's start with why you called for an appointment."

"My wife and I have been together for the past 20 years. We got married ten years ago," she said. "It's my second marriage. God knows why I married the first time. I was too young. I was just out of college and back then, I thought that my boyfriend had his head on straight. I had big plans for myself after college, but my father and mother saw my education as a way to find a husband, and they encouraged me to marry him. So I did. That's the way it was. Back then, I didn't see that I had a choice, but I certainly think I do now."

She continued. "Anyway, we got married after graduation and we moved to Oklahoma City where he's from. That marriage only lasted two years before I knew I had to get out in order not to lose myself. Otherwise I was destined to be nothing more than a wife and homemaker. I also realized in those years, that I was attracted to, and wanted to be with, women."

While Elsa spoke, I sensed a hint of tears behind her eyes, but it was clear that she had long perfected the art of suppressing her emotions with a reflexive smile.

"My wife has always handled the finances, but now I want to be a part of those decisions," she said. "The problem is that I am unable to." She hesitated. "Maybe I shouldn't complain about her since no marriage is perfect. I suppose I have nothing to worry about."

All couples negotiate the realities of financial decision-making, whether they actively or passively establish an arrangement. Elsa wanted to be more involved in the financial decision-making process, but it seemed to shake up their established norm.

I asked, "When you say you are 'unable to' what exactly does that mean?"

Elsa deflected my question. She replied, "We have an amazing marriage!"

I wasn't sure who Elsa was trying to convince—herself or me.

Because financial therapy is my area of expertise, I am accustomed to hearing about couples' financial arrangements. I help people understand their emotions and personal beliefs that drive their financial actions and decisions. Clients like Elsa reach out for help when their conflicts become too much to handle or resolve on their own.

Elsa described their marriage as traditional, which to her meant, "My wife handles the finances and I handle everything else."

A couple or individual's financial arrangement is personal. What matters to me as the therapist, is how I can most successfully help my clients understand their choices and decision-making processes. Elsa struck me as a strong-willed, educated, and independent businesswoman. Her marriage might have been traditional by her account, but nothing about Elsa's personality felt "traditional" to me.

She said, "My wife makes all of the financial decisions and handles the paperwork, the taxes and the investments. But when I have questions about an investment account or the taxes, she yells at me to mind my own business and that I'm insulting her intelligence or questioning her ability."

As Elsa continued to describe her wife's behavior, she became defensive. "You don't understand. We have an amazing marriage even if the sex is..."

I waited for Elsa to finish her thought but her voice trailed off and a heavy silence hung between us. I made a mental note to return to this place, but not yet. For now, I changed the conversation. I said, "You're correct, no marriage is perfect. Had you professed sheer perfection I would be more worried than I currently am!"

My emphasis was intentional. I now had Elsa's attention, although she was still defensive.

She replied, "Worried? What are you worried about? I think you're being a tad alarmist."

I responded, "Well, perhaps there is nothing to be alarmed about. However, I'd rather you get angry at me for sounding a false alarm than not prompt you to take action to avoid a potential financial crisis." Without pause, and for effect, I returned to Elsa's unfinished sentence. "You were about to say something about your sex life. What was it?"

I turned the focus back to her comment on sex because financial abuse rarely exists in a vacuum, and the spouse or partner often shields their financial rage within some subtle or covert form of sexual rage, guilt, and shame. I needed more information about Elsa's marriage before I jumped to any conclusions about their sex life, and since I had already sounded the alarm bells for potential financial control, I needed to first ascertain if the sex to which Elsa hinted was intense but consensual, or controlling and aggressive.

Professionals who specialize in trauma and addiction must tend to the meaning of a client's experience before assigning a pathological lens. For many clients like Elsa, talking about sex is difficult, but it was her intonation and inflection on the word *even* when she said, "...even if the sex is..." that caught my attention. Was her hesitation due to her embarrassment about sex or indicative of something more troubling?

EROTICIZED RAGE:
WHEN SEX BECOMES A WEAPON

Sex is a powerful word, particularly in the context of therapy. When an individual or a couple introduces sex into a session, I try to ascertain what sex means for them. Is sex a way to feel connection or fulfill excitement? Do they prefer novelty and risky sex, or consistency and sexual safety?

Psychotherapist and author Esther Perel frames the puzzle this way. "[Is sex] a time when you don't always have to be responsible, and adult, and mature? Is it a kind of a safe way where you can regress and be taken care of and surrender? Is it the place where you can actually safely feel powerful when you don't always feel in other parts of your life? What does sex mean to you?"[3]

Erotic sex is a uniquely human experience that can be powerful in its intimacy. Erotic sex, however, is something entirely different from sexual intensity that is used as a weapon. When sexual intensity is used to overpower or control, it's a sign of Eroticized Rage—a sexual arousal pattern that fuses sex, shame, and covert or overt levels of rage. This type of sexual behavior often involves entitlement and some form of humiliation, revenge, and retaliation:

- Humiliation—Acting out old betrayals and abuse
- Revenge—Acting out old betrayals and abuse
- Retaliation—Employs sex as retribution for perceived harm

The elements of Eroticized Rage are employed and experienced differently in each relationship. Take a moment to consider what role each person has in the following power dynamic:

• **Renee** is 22 and met Kai online. After they both "swiped right," they texted a few times and agreed to meet. Before their meet up, Renee promised her roommate that no matter what, she would not hook up with Kai. When Renee came home, she confessed. "He totally put me down. He said, there's no way you can be as smart as you say—you're too good looking." However, despite Kai's verbal denigration, Renee still went back to his place to have sex.

• **Melanie and Scott** have been married for fifteen years. Often, when they are out with friends, Scott finds something about Melanie's behavior to attack. He quickly follows with an additional comment that Melanie is so sensitive. Everyone laughs. Back at the house, Scott tells Melanie that the best thing she can do to get over her hypersensitivity is to have sex with him. She feels dismissed and humiliated, but she complies.

• **Louise** is in her early 30s. She seeks therapy to address her low sex drive and libido. One month earlier, she'd given birth to their first child. Louise shares that her husband often tells her that he prefers her sexier pre-pregnancy body. She says, "He reminds me to watch what I eat and tells me to keep sexually active so that I feel good about myself. I'm really grateful. There must be something wrong with my libido."

- **Aria and her husband** have sex every night before they fall asleep. Despite the fact that on many weeknights she is exhausted, Aria obliges him in order to silence his demands. She also knows that if he doesn't get his way he punishes her by refusing to speak to her the next morning. She thinks it's just easier to say yes to get along.

In all of the previous examples, sex is used in overt or covert ways to restore a loss of power or as a way to compensate for shame, insecurity, and emotional or psychological vulnerability. The elements of humiliation, revenge, and retaliation are experienced differently in each behavior pattern, yet are inherent to each sexual arousal template to exploit a victim.

Sexual arousal templates are forged in early childhood and adolescence, and consist of our history and genetic blueprint, thoughts, feelings, and experiences. The introduction of stressors and trauma increases the release of stress hormones and neurochemicals such as fear, pain, or anger. Thus, early childhood and developmental experience can become consciously and unconsciously linked with intense emotions.

SEXUAL PAIN AS PLEASURE

Arousal that originates in childhood can be sexually reenacted in adult life, but it is important to note that not all sexual arousal that involves pain or anger is a trauma reenactment. When sexual domination and control are part of healthy kink/fetish play, it is a way to channel aggression. Wherein intense emotions and desires may be too uncomfortable, for some, the novelty of power dynamics in BDSM can offer a sexually safe release.[4]

Psychotherapist and author Dr. Robert Weiss, LCSW, recently described healthy sexual expression in this way: "All of us, to some degree, bring our aggressions (and passivities) into our sexual lives in small ways and large. If dominance and rage are an integrated part of someone's sexual arousal template, there are plenty of consensual, highly satisfying ways to meet this need/desire. As long as what's acted out is not disrespectful nor distressing to either partner and is carried out with the full consent and awareness of all parties, it is potentially not a problem."[5]

Rage and anger become problematic in the absence of consent before, during, and after sexual play. Consent entails prior agreements or conversations ensuring safety and respect. If the infliction of pain or shame is the intended end goal a problem exits.

Pornography is one of a few topics that provoke visceral negative and positive reactions, but it's typically about the content or how the content is being used. When pornography is used as a part of an individual or couple's sexual repertoire, it is critical that its inclusion be part of consensual sex. Any argument in favor of pornography fails in the case of revenge porn, cyber bullying, or cyber sexual harassment.[6] In such cases there is a clear absence of consent before and during sex, and sex is being used as a weapon to settle an imbalance of power.

Consider the partner who seeks revenge for being sexually rejected: A wife who feels insecure because her husband earns the majority of the money and threatens to leave the marriage. An affair partner who finds ways to publicly humiliate her married sexual partner by uploading secret photos taken during sex. A husband who feels justified posting his wife's nude photos online because of her infidelity in the marriage.

Sexual revenge and retribution to humiliate the victim is simply a means to an end. Those elements of Eroticized Rage as restoration of self-worth and esteem are fundamental to the sexual exploitation of a victim.

DAVE'S STORY REVISITED

We first read about Dave in Chapter Five. His partners know him to be emotionally abusive, but his manipulation and abuse is concealed behind a veneer of grandiosity and charm.

Dave began to date shortly after he divorced, and framed the divorce as an unfortunate result of his wife's drinking and lack of affection. As Dave told it, "Divorce wasn't what I wanted. I had hoped to stay married for a long time." He enjoyed the public sympathy that his narrative garnered. He played on the emotions of unsuspecting women who trusted that his marital demise was the result of two people falling out of love.

Dave didn't share that his wife wanted to return to work after raising their 20-year-old daughter, and that this shift in their marriage exposed his insecurity and sadistic need for control. She left a successful career as a business coach to raise their daughter, who was now establishing her own life.

Over a period of several months, Dave inflicted his narcissistic rage on his wife with increasing violence and sexual aggression. He attempted to cut off her access to their joint bank account, at which point she left and filed for divorce. Dave was focused and ruthless in his sadistic psychological campaign, carried out behind a well-cultivated veil of charm and normalcy.

Dave's wife left after his monetary control escalated and filed for divorce. For her, it became the point at which she could no longer tolerate the intolerable. Making a determination about self-care and what is or isn't tolerable in an abusive relationship is a personal decision based on distinct circumstances. No two cases are the same and each will require different levels of careful discernment.

DETERMINING WHEN TO LEAVE

Domestic violence and varying levels of abuse will always culminate in negative consequences for the victim unless a perpetrator changes their behavior or the victim leaves. In the direst cases, a victim cannot find enough safety or enough distance to prevent the perpetrator's murderous assaults.

Consider Elsa's case: she chose to stay in her marriage and work on shifting their imbalance of power in an attempt to confront her wife's control of the finances. She believed there was not yet sufficient threat to warrant her leaving, or for me to alert the authorities—the operative word being *yet*.

MONETIZED RAGE

The #MeToo movement shined a light on sexual exploitation, but the movement also highlighted the more hidden, yet equally devastating dynamics of Monetized Rage—a term I introduced in *For Love and Money* to define financial abuse fueled by covert or overt levels of rage and shame, that utilizes financial means to control and exploit.[7]

When Elsa described her situation, I recognized the telltale signs of Monetized Rage. This type of abuse is often intimately related to sexual exploitation, and has a potentially destructive or ruinous financial outcome for the victim. Whereas Eroticized Rage exploits and controls with anger, sex and shame, Monetized Rage uses money to control and exploit. Both forms of rage use entitlement, anger, or violence to control and exploit. It is important to determine if there is evidence of sexual and/or financial abuse in your relationship to shift the balance of power.

The greatest risk to the victim of Monetized Rage is that the damage may be beyond repair by the time the abuse becomes too obvious to ignore or the victim is ready to take action, at which point the victim has lost precious time or the opportunity to intervene.

WHAT ARE THE WARNING SIGNS OF MONETIZED RAGE?

- **Revenge**: Limiting or cutting off an individual's access to finances. This is accompanied by intimidation and/or a threat to obstruct access to money or withhold financial support. The threat can also involve a forced sexual demand for financial gain or used as a way for the victim to "make things right." This implies that the victim is at fault and can rectify the perceived slight or rejection by giving in.

- **Humiliation**: This involves some form of sexual humiliation along with a threat of financial retaliation. The person's intention is to shame, diminish, or denigrate the victim's sense of self. This tactic might involve subtle but effective public humiliation, or private acts of rage.

- **Retaliation**: An individual might spend money in order to financially strap the victim. This retribution may be for a perceived slight or rejection of sexual advances, and involves the threat of public sexual exposure. The victim's access to funds may be based on implied sexual performance or satisfaction.

The vast majority of couples who have money conflicts are able to shift and flex with changing financial needs, though the path may create a rocky relationship or require a professional's help. Numerous studies suggest that unresolved conflicts about money pose the greatest risk for relationship distress or divorce. A 2018 study reported in the *Journal of Financial Therapy* found that, "…Couples who pay their bills in a less structured manner are more likely than those with a more established budget and plan to keep a financial secret from their partner."[8]

Elsa was only beginning to recognize that her wife's behavior was more than an established plan—it was exploitative. However, it can be nearly impossible to detect abuse or exploitation, much less be proactive about it, when the abuse is absent of glaring indicators or alarms. Most relationships are an intricate pas-de-deux, and are danced almost exclusively behind closed doors. As was the case with Elsa, it is nearly impossible for one to comprehend the reality of a situation without the introduction of critical objectivity. She was the victim of Monetized Rage, masked by her wife's thinly veiled sexual aggression.

PERRY AND CELESTE

Perry and Celeste are a fictional couple in the HBO miniseries *Big Little Lies*, adapted from the novel by Liane Moriarty. Their marital dynamic is similar to Dave's story in its graphic depiction of sexual and financial abuse and power dynamics in a relationship.

Celeste was a successful attorney before she gave up her career to marry Perry and raise their children. Their marriage seems perfect: Celeste has two beautiful boys, an adoring husband, and leads an enviable life, but their seemingly idyllic marriage conceals a pattern of domestic violence that begins with emotional and physical abuse that culminates in rape.

Perry's violence toward Celeste takes a sadistic turn when Celeste reveals her desire to return to work. It is at this point that his eroticized narcissistic insecurity of losing Celeste escalates.

Despite Celeste's previous success in her career and strong public persona, behind closed doors she maintains a submissive One Down position in the marriage and endures sexual humiliation and rape. This power reversal is in sharp contrast to Perry's sexual and financial control over Celeste that is driven by his insecurity and fear of losing her. Both use sexual intensity and violence to restore power and control.

There is much to explore in this couple's dynamic. Their collective and individual attempts to restore power are reenacted through sexual intensity and rage. We learn that Perry and Celeste experienced trauma in their past, albeit differently, and in ways that led to their dyadic reenactment of Eroticized and Monetized Rage.

Perry and Celeste begin couples counseling to discuss Perry's anger and the escalation in their sexual intensity. When the couple alludes to sexual abuse within their cycle of sexual intensity, the therapist registers appropriate concern. It is at the insistence of her therapist in the wake of escalating violence that Celeste plans to take their boys and leave Perry.

People like Elsa's wife or Dave, who both have deep narcissistic wounds, typically deny having a problem. They are unlikely to seek help for it. In many cases, it is the distressed partner, like Elsa or Celeste, who seeks support, and with whom the therapist attempts to break through denial.

In relationships where sexual arousal involves humiliation or degradation, it is important to understand whether these dynamics are part of a healthy, mutually pleasurable sex life, or a more serious traumatic reenactment leading to denigration of self or humiliation of another.

DETERMINING NEXT STEPS

In the presence of exploitation and control, knowing what action to take is critical for change. Action can mean that both partners work together to change their dynamic toward a mutually defined goal. Mutual work leads to increased intimacy and an increase in empathic attunement in the relationship. The outcome can be nothing short of awesome.

If you identify as a victim of Eroticized or Monetized Rage, consider the following questions for yourself or someone you love:

- What degree of change is realistic in this relationship?
- What are my boundaries to determine whether I stay in or leave the relationship?
- What evidence is there that the person doing the exploiting wants to change?
- What are the risks of staying?

If imminent danger to self or others exists, it may be necessary to leave the relationship. Action in that case means exiting the situation as quickly as possible. The items below will help you begin the change process toward self-empowerment.

ACTION REQUIRES H.E.L.P.

- **GET HELP!** Hope is not a back-up plan. Many victims of this abuse avoid responsibility in the hope that what is happening will somehow change on its own. The best course of action is action, not inaction. Find a professional—an accountant, attorney, or therapist—for financial, legal, or psychological help.
- **EMPOWER** Yourself: Work to build your self-esteem and self-worth. Surround yourself with supportive friends, relatives, or a therapist who will remind you of strengths, not weaknesses. Take in others' positive

regard. In times of self-doubt, remind yourself that those who care can't all be wrong. Tap into and embrace authentic accomplishments rather than focusing on the negatives. To empower oneself means to relinquish the shameful and One Down position.

- LEARN: Educate yourself about finances and your financial situation. Financial and legal professionals can help restore the inequalities so that there is mutual respect in the financial arrangement.
- PROTECT YOURSELF: Set boundaries for self-empowerment and relational balance. Learn practices, tools, and principles inherent to a healthy relationship that lead to a healthier monetary, sexual, and relational wellbeing.

Earlier in the book, I challenged you, the reader, to consider the concept of power as you experienced it in your childhood, specifically: Who had power over you? If it was your parent or caregiver, did they abuse their power? Conversely, if you are a parent or a caregiver to your own parent, how does power factor into that dynamic?

Throughout our exploration, we examined dynamics between parent and child and how, in those relationships, we experienced power. We looked at personality and character, and the ways in which our family system taught true and false power. Without a healthy environment in which to flourish, a false self may have developed to protect one's insecurities. In those cases, we learned how buried shame and narcissistic ego wounds manifest. That started our foray into the darker side of personality, power, and control.

Now, consider your current professional and romantic relationships.

- When do you feel most and least powerful?
- How do you express power in your relationships?
- What do you value most in a relationship?
- When considered in tandem, are sex and money an issue for you? If so, how?

These questions and the essential skills to promote personal influence and self-empowerment are the focus of our next chapter, *Leveling the Playing Field*.

CHAPTER SEVEN

LEVELING THE PLAYING FIELD

Every human has four endowments – self-awareness,
conscience, independent will and creative imagination.
These give us the ultimate human freedom...
The power to choose, to respond, to change.

— Stephen Covey

Mutuality in a relationship means different things to different people. Mutuality requires an openness to influence, emotional availability, and an understanding that both partners have needs that matter. This is the high-water mark for most if not all relationships, and in the best of all possible worlds, each person is willing and able to strive for this level of mutuality.

A fundamental reality for many romantic relationships is that there exists an imbalance of power. You would not have chosen this book or read this far if it wasn't true for you or someone you know. Partners may perceive themselves or the other as having more power and influence or access to resources. The relationship may be one-sided due to a partner's lack of emotional availability or vulnerability. All of these aspects of a relationship create imbalances of power and control.

A 2016 study published in the *Personality and Social Psychology Bulletin* presented two different concepts of power—power as influence and power as autonomy.[1] Researchers found that people often seek power not to exert control over others, but to be the master of their own fate. I wonder if that's why Greek myths continue to be so enduringly compelling. Like these characters, each of us seeks to be the master of our own fate.

Self-empowerment is the underlying motivation of this book and is the focus of this chapter: how the less powerful partner (perceived by self or other) can establish a greater sense of power as autonomy, resist influence, and flip the imbalance of power. To do so, they must be willing and able to assert themselves, recognize their personal attributes, and value their worth in the relationship. This reminds me of Rebecca with whom I worked several years ago. Her struggle illustrates the uncertain but triumphant journey to self-empowerment.

REBECCA

Rebecca came to therapy to understand why she stayed in her marriage. At the time of her first visit, she had been married for over fifteen years. For the last ten of those years, her husband didn't bother to hide his affairs, he flaunted them. Rebecca wanted to address what she referred to as her "utter lack of self-respect." Her internal conflict was the problem she wished to address.

She said, "My husband cheats. I know he has affairs— some emotional and some sexual. I'm clearly unhappy, but I stay. What self-respecting person would put up with this?"

Rebecca reported that there was no violence or threat of financial reprisal if she left. They had two children; one in middle school and one in high school, both of whom she hoped one day would go off to college. "Maybe," she said. "I'll divorce him once they're out of the house."

It is common for parents to stay together for the sake of the children and then divorce once the nest is empty, or if the marriage evaporates after they're gone. Rebecca was making a conscious and informed choice. She knew about many of her husband's affairs, and yet chose to stay. The question she wanted to work through was why she wouldn't leave him.

I empathized with Rebecca, and told her, "I understand that you feel stuck and I can really see how frustrated you are. I think it might be more helpful to examine the benefits of staying in the marriage rather than the costs of leaving." Her eyes locked onto mine. I wanted to help Rebecca verbalize any unrealized motivation for her choice. It is human nature to seek pleasure or avoid pain. Clearly, Rebecca was avoiding the pain of divorce by not leaving, and while she felt little-to-no pleasure being married, there clearly was a payoff or a benefit to staying.

She began counting the benefits aloud. "I work, and I feel proud about my job. I was able to stay home with my children when they were younger. Now they need me less, but I am still available to pick them up from their activities and be there for them. I don't need to worry about money. We live in a comfortable house. My children get to live in a stable home until they leave for college."

It was the last one that captured her attention.

"If I leave, I'm afraid that I won't be able to financial-ly provide for their college on my own, and I'm afraid that their father won't pay for them if we divorce. I'm staying because I know he doesn't value education like I do, and I want them to be able to go to college if they choose to do so."

Most of my clients don't always have such a clean and easy path to awareness, but we had been working together for a while, and it seemed that Rebecca was ready to con-nect the dots. She was clear about her reasons for staying in the marriage: to ensure her children's education and well-being, even if it was at the expense of her own hap-piness. Rebecca's marriage was unfulfilling and void of pleasure, but her situation was neither dire nor financially exploitive.

You could say that Rebecca was fortunate, in that her decision to stay did not involve imminent danger. Her choice may not be a decision that other partners are willing to make. Nonetheless, Rebecca made an informed decision based on an outcome that she was willing to live with.

In our work, Rebecca focused on her strengths and built her self-esteem to advocate for herself and her children. She grew confident that she would thrive in her life—with or without her husband. Rebecca became her most ardent advocate. Most importantly, Rebecca went from passive to active protector of her children.

The path to self-empowerment isn't always clear—it can be daunting. Harnessing our personal autonomy will foster personal success.

RELATIONAL CURRENCY

In a relationship we each bring symbols and acts to communicate our affection, love, and commitment to the other. I call this **relational currency**. How we convey this currency to our loved ones differs from person to person. We can also understand relational currency to mean the value each partner assigns to the relationship and those acts or statements. For example, folding the clothes or picking up a spouse's favorite dessert are gestures of affection and love, as are physical displays of affection. Consider the following:

- What are my relational strengths?
- What uniqueness do I bring to the table, relationally?
- How do I choose to communicate this to my loved one?
- Am I willing to be honest with myself?

For some, relational currency may be providing income or access to financial resources. A partner who depends on those resources may not be able to contribute to the relationship in that way, but in return can provide their own currency of love, affection, or emotional availability, a valued resource that is often in short supply.

Several thoughts from *For Love and Money* are apropos:

Currency is generally thought of as a form of economic or monetary exchange (i.e., money), but currency needn't be legal tender. Currency can also be the emotional and sexual cache a person brings to a relationship. This type of relational currency speaks to what we value, our relational strengths, and the ways in which we communicate our values and strengths to a loved one.

In the early phase of connection, we don't dive into the proverbial life questions. We come together under an emotional and erotic cosmic trance, which we know from previous chapters as limerence, and we are not likely to ask the deeper introspective questions, such as, What do I value most about being in a relationship? This is because our brains are hijacked by the hormonal and chemical rush of lust and attraction. Eventually, these questions surface after limerence subsides, and the rose-colored glasses come off under a cloud of exasperation or relational disconnect.

Consider these questions:

- How does my partner express love and affection?
- What does my partner value in the relationship?
- In what ways does my partner show up in our relationship?

Modeling **emotional availability** and being **emotionally vulnerable** increases the level of intimacy and respect in a coupleship. Sexual and emotional intimacy can have the greatest immediate impact on the power differential in a relationship. Being emotionally present and asking for emotional availability from your partner may be a difficult proposition. It isn't everyone's strength—it wasn't one for Alex.

ALEX

Alex is an aggressive negotiator. His bold, unflappable appearance makes him a tactical threat in business and he wields it with force to crush the competition. That tactic serves him well in his profession, but it has failed him mightily in his marriage and personal relationships.

Alex started therapy one year ago after he and his wife, Ella, had a marital crisis that began with a make-or-break argument. She insisted that he go to therapy, insinuating that he was the problem. Alex begrudgingly made an appointment, not because he agreed but rather because he felt he could finally "prove her wrong."

In that initial session, Alex confidently shared that his foray into therapy would be short lived. He began to lobby for my approval by launching into the details of their argument.

"I know I'm not perfect, but my wife is the one who needs to be here, not me!"

"That might also be the case, but I'm glad that you are here." I said. "However, why do you think she needs to be here and not you," I asked?

"Because! She says it's me who is the problem and that I'm wrong!"

I didn't doubt that Alex believed he had no shared responsibility in their marital tension. I thought back to Ben, who we met in Chapter Five. Both men were similar in that neither of them took responsibility for their circumstances. However, unlike Ben, I believed that if Alex stayed in therapy, he could tolerate hearing a different perspective.

I resisted falling into the classic trap of taking sides in their argument thereby encouraging his right-wrong; all-or-nothing thinking. Instead, I focused on what seemed to be a more productive therapeutic vein to mine; the power dynamic in their marriage. If my instinct was correct, Alex would see the difference between strength versus force, and shift their imbalance of power.

Since then, Alex had made a good deal of progress in therapy. However, this day he arrived to our session agitated. He reported that he hadn't stood up to Ella during an argument the week before. He sat on the couch and vacillated between brooding silence and self-directed frustration.

Alex had learned a lot about himself and how to counter his natural inclination to avoid conflict or emotional intimacy. He might have been frustrated with himself for his lack of confidence in their argument. I was delighted that his new behavior was to remain relational and not avoid conflict.

He told me, "I didn't know why, but Ella was clearly angry with me, so I asked her what was wrong. You just know these things, you know? After so many years of marriage, I could tell something was up!"

Alex winced. He said, "I asked her nicely, 'Ella. Is something the matter?' She said no. She then walked out of the kitchen and went upstairs into the bedroom. I gave her some time before I went in and saw her laying on the bed crying."

"So far so good, Alex," I said. You didn't avoid an unfinished conversation. Instead, you went into the bedroom and confronted your own feelings in addition to confronting the issue. Most importantly, you didn't blow up at her or avoid the issue for it to blow up on you later."

"Yeah, well, I didn't do me or Ella any favors," he confessed. "It would have been better had I gone into my office instead of going into the bedroom, because that's when she went ballistic. I don't get it. When should I try to talk, and when should I just let her be? I obviously made things worse by talking!"

"I doubt you made things worse by talking," I told him. "Emotions can cause discomfort, and it is your pattern to avoid them, thus avoiding conflict. But this friction can only be resolved by talking. You chose to have a difficult conversation instead of kicking it down the road. Let's look at what happens when you avoid these issues."

He said, "I get it, I get it! I've been coming here long enough that something is soaking in. Nothing good has ever come from avoiding her, but I just can't take it when she's so reactive. I know I'm better than I used to be. In the past, I would have left the house or disappeared into my office, but this time was no better. I just stood there and didn't move."

Alex became indignant. "I wish she would just deal with her own anger and stop making me the problem, then we would have had a better evening. Her emotions are not my problem! I don't know. I have never felt more powerless than I do in this marriage."

I waited in silence, letting Alex sit under the weight of his discomfort and the truth of his words. Alex said he felt "powerless." When we're ready, awareness of what makes us most uncomfortable can be transformed into productive insight. In this way, silence is not just poetic gold; it's a powerful tool.

HARNESSING YOUR POWER

Just when we think that our partner or something about them is our obstacle, rest assured—they are not the problem, we are. The path through an emotional choke point is self-empowerment. The power that we derive from believing in ourselves is on par with caring about others without forsaking self.

Alex was no stranger to obstacles. He built a career on the ashes of his impediments. He was a man who prided himself on being bold and unflappable under pressure. I believe that his powerlessness had more to do with his nervous system than a reluctance to face conflict. Alex survived his childhood by being tough and fighting his way out of trouble. As a child of an alcoholic, he flew below the radar to escape his mother's alcohol-fueled rage.

I understood why Alex was disappointed in himself. His survival and business success depended on his brawn and intellect, which failed him in the moment when his wife was hurting. In stressful or threatening situations, our biological and largely involuntary fear response is activated. During an argument with his wife—or one that Alex hoped to avoid—his nervous system's *fight, flight or freeze* response kicked in. Alex's brain and nervous system perceived that this argument—although far from life threatening—was a significant threat, and he became overwhelmed.

What Alex needed was to cobble together his heart and his head like Frankenstein's monster; marrying logic with emotion. Maybe more than anything, Alex simply needed self-compassion, which therapy could provide for him until he was able to provide it for himself.

FIGHT, FLIGHT, OR FREEZE

Alex's conflict patterns with Ella echoed two of the three threat responses: flight: *I would have left the house or disappeared into my office,* and freeze: *But this time was no better. I just stood there and didn't move.*

I shared my observations with Alex, after which, he stood up and started to swing his arms in a circular motion as he paced around the room. He was using a self-soothing technique we have practiced to regulate his nervous system—a type of "shake-off," similar to how animals naturally discharge stress after a life-threatening event— only now he used it to interrupt feeling powerless and to move into action.

EMOTIONAL THAW

Alex may have been disappointed in himself, but months of therapy were having their intended effect. He was in what I call the "emotional thaw"—the softening of (conscious and/or unconscious) defenses meant to protect our vulnerable underbelly. This was good news and I was happy for Alex. The more he felt his emotions, the more empowered he would be in the face of conflict. That is a superpower.

I waited for Alex to look up. I wanted eye contact to emphasize what I was about to say.

"Alex, feeling powerless is not the same as abdicating your power."

He responded, "What do you mean? How am I abdicating my power? That makes no sense."

I asked, "Do you abdicate your power, you know, give your power away—to Ella, for example?"

Alex shot me an angry glance. I shot back a nonverbal, *Hey, I'm just sayin'*, that spoke volumes and broke the tension. To borrow a line from William Ury, co-founder of Harvard's Program on Negotiation, "Being honest and straight with people can work well if you accompany the candor with empathy and respect." He also said, "Be hard on the problem, not the person."[2]

I am careful with Alex, as I am with all my clients. We had worked together long enough that Alex knew I was well intentioned. I shared with him that I deeply respect his conviction to change. I also enjoyed his wry sense of humor, which surfaces—as it had in that moment—when he is most frustrated. My question, "Do you abdicate your power?" was an invitation for Alex to look inward. He was only beginning to understand that his anger—though misdirected at me—was meant for what resonated as true; akin to the phrase, "shooting the messenger."

Alex relaxed and smiled, but before we closed our session, I circled back to something he said earlier. I said, "You're right that Ella's emotions aren't your responsibility. That said, if you're willing, you can still extend compassion at a relatively low risk to your own power."

EMOTIONS AS POWER

There are several ways to successfully harness power, beginning with our emotions. Dr. Lisa Feldman Barrett, a neuroscientist at Northeastern University and the author of *How Emotions Are Made,* writes that we have more control over and responsibility for our emotions than many people believe. At the center of her work is a sensory process of the human nervous system called interoception. This sensory process helps us understand and feel what is going on inside our bodies, and how we experience our sensations as emotion.

According to Barrett, "[Interoception] demonstrates that you're not at the mercy of emotions that arise unbidden to control your behavior. You are an architect of these experiences. Your river of feelings might feel like it's flowing over you, but actually you're the river's source."[3] Interoception is a fundamental feature of our nervous system that remains a mystery of science. However, Alex doesn't need to wait for science. Anyone can harness the power of their emotions, resist influence and control of others, and take an essential step toward self-empowerment: to pause when agitated.

I learned this the hard way.

Years ago, before the days of email marketing software, a close friend sent out a mass email to announce her company's new logo. Almost immediately, I began receiving "Reply All" responses congratulating the partners on their big news. I was annoyed with the senseless "Reply Alls." Sure, I could have ignored the emails—or, better yet, not been so arrogant and recognized that everyone was celebrating my friend. However, I dashed off my own *Please do not "Reply All"* email. Within seconds, my friend called. Unlike me, she was gracious. Instead of being insulted or angry, she playfully chided me for being so brusque. She was right. Her grace taught me an invaluable life lesson: *Step away from the keyboard.* This phrase became my forever mantra to remind myself to pause when agitated before I do something rash, or that I might regret.

To Pause Is Power

There are physiological processes at work when we *step away from the keyboard* and take a pause. That time-out drives a wedge between our primal brain (fear response) and modern brain (frontal cortex). This pause allows the heart rate to slow down, the muscles to relax from their fight or flight stance, and the prefrontal cortex to come back online to allow clearer thinking after it's been effectively hijacked by fear. The reality is that our brains do not focus or function well enough to make good decisions when we are in a reactive state.

Boundaries as Power

The term "boundaries" is frequently used in popular culture, but there is some confusion about what that actually means. Boundaries are the core of healthy communication and relationships. As a therapist, I have found boundaries to be one of the hardest acts of self-care.

What defines a boundary? How is a boundary established and expressed? How are boundaries maintained? Perhaps most perplexing, what should be done when a boundary is ignored or breached? Becoming familiar with these questions is fundamental to self-empowerment.

Boundaries can be physical, sexual, and verbal. In the simplest of descriptions, a front door to a house is a physical boundary. When the front door is locked, it is an indication that a prompt is necessary for those inside to *choose* to open the door. It's a choice, unless it's an invasion, and then we are no longer talking about boundaries, but rather attack or assault.

The same principles apply for sexual boundaries. The space between where you end and your partner begins is a boundary. Boundaries provide both protection—communicating your preference for distance or proximity, and containment—controlling your distance or proximity. You have a right to choose with whom you will be sexual and to whom you express your sexual energy or contact. Sex without consent, as is addressed throughout this book, is assault or rape.

Boundaries become confusing with speaking and listening. When you share your thoughts or words with someone, it is important to contain what you say and monitor how you say it. Our words and the way we same them matter.

Former FBI hostage negotiator and author Chris Voss learned to choose his words and deliver them wisely, because in his line of work, lives were on the line. To hear Voss say it, "No one likes anybody who is blunt, everybody likes a straight shooter. What's the difference? A straight shooter is careful how it lands."[4] In this way, Voss needed to be a straight shooter and not make promises to a hostage taker if he couldn't deliver. At the same time, he needed to be careful with his words to de-escalate the tension of the situation. It's the same for William Ury, co-founder of Harvard's Program on Negotiation. He negotiates civil conflicts and teaches negotiation tactics to leaders in government and business.

Perhaps the most difficult part of boundaries is when we are listening. On this side of a conversation, we choose what we take in and either respond or react to what we are hearing. One of my favorite aphorisms credited to Eleanor Roosevelt is: *No one can make you feel inferior without your consent.* The maxim is powerful and a testament to this point.

If someone I know walked up to me and said, "Deb, you are short and ignorant," I might have many feelings about those two observations. If I do not react immediately and instead consider the statement for a moment, I can agree and reply, "Yes, I am short." I have a choice regarding the statement about my intelligence. I can agree, "Yes, that is true, I am ignorant," or I can disagree with the statement, "No, that is false." Once I engage my protective listening boundaries, I slow or interrupt my fight or flight response. I am empowered and in control of emotions and can resist influence.

BODY LANGUAGE

These same boundaries apply to nonverbal communication. A message that is conveyed through facial expressions or body language registers through our eyes and into the nervous system. As infants, we used our senses to process information long before we had words at our disposal. This sensory learning became encoded into our memories as implicitly (and eventually, explicitly) learned information. We knew exactly what receiving a glance, or *that look,* from a loved one meant.

The power of body language is personified in *Fearless Girl,* the diminutive yet fierce 50-inch bronze statue in lower Manhattan's financial district.[5] *Fearless Girl* was privately commissioned and put in place March 2017, to celebrate International Women's Day. She stands strong, with her mighty legs firmly rooted, hands on her hips and chin held high. Her original placement was set in a face-off with *Charging Bull,* the iconic bronze sculpture symbolizing Wall Street. Although she was eventually moved to a different location, *Fearless Girl's* daring stance in juxtaposition to *Charging Bull* became a global sensation and remains a symbol of female empowerment.

In an open letter to New York City Mayor, Bill de Blasio, Letitia James, then Public Advocate and now Attorney General of New York, wrote, "Fearless Girl stands as a powerful beacon, showing women—young and old—that no dream is too big and no ceiling is too high."

It is almost impossible to not be moved by *Fearless Girl's* powerful magnificence—her bronze body symbolizing the infinite power of human determination.

INFORMATION IS POWER

While one partner may be responsible for a relationship's financial or sexual decisions, both partners must be equally involved in the decision-making process. The meaning of equality looks different for each relationship, but healthy relationships are built on empowered partners—not indifference or avoidance.

Let's revisit a statement from Chapter Five: *Hope is not a back-up plan. Many victims of this abuse avoid responsibility in the hope that what is happening will somehow change on its own.* The best course of action is action, not inaction. Again, I recommend that you *find a professional—an accountant, attorney, or therapist—for financial, legal or psychological help.* This directive in the "H" in H.E.L.P. is wise, and taking action is vital for self-empowerment. However, there is more to be done. There are three facets to using information as power.

Facet #1 – Obtaining Information is Power

This is where legal or financial professionals come in. They know how to find the information that you need and can help explain where you can access it. This involves accountants, legal professionals, online finance programs, and other paraprofessional groups to assist in financial education.

In *For Love and Money*, many readers resonated with one passage in particular: "The ways in which partners and spouses are willing to "show up" or be emotionally present and engaged with each other (and themselves) often points to the heart of relational disputes. As I often tell my clients, **there is the information we need but do not ask for, and the information we already have, yet choose to ignore**. The arrangement that couples script are laden with spoken agreements and silent arrangements, to themselves or to another. And the struggles many couples experience are the direct result of these conscious decisions made or avoided."

In addition, the twelve-step programs can provide

a wealth of information. Millions of people have accessed the wisdom and collective strength in such programs. Debtors Anonymous, Spenders Anonymous, and Underearners Anonymous all offer rich resources to work on self-empowerment and can help free individuals from the crushing forces of debt, spending, and under earning. These issues are rooted in shame, feeling less-than, or a sense of being not good enough.

FACET #2 – ACCESS TO INFORMATION IS POWER

Having access to information is equally important to getting the information. Consider in your relationship whether you are being denied access to relevant information. As noted earlier, action might require immediately leaving a relationship if there is imminent danger to self or others. In those cases, action means exiting as quickly as possible. Avoid the "Triple Ds:" *Doubling Down on Denial*—the deluded belief that the situation will get better.

A spouse or partner who withholds, denies, manipulates, distorts, or conceals information wields tremendous power and influence; yet their influence may only be an illusion. Influence exists because a person grants them with perceived power and entitlement. A vulnerable person will remain *falsely* disempowered as long as they *falsely* empower their partner.

Think about your relationships:

- Is information shared, or is it withheld?
- How easy is it to obtain information? If it is easily obtained, why? If not, why not?

- Does your partner use their power to deny, manipulate, distort, or conceal information?
- Where possible, develop a strategy to reduce someone else's illegitimate use of power over you.

FACET #3 – KNOW WHAT TO DO WITH INFORMATION

The third facet is about knowing what to do with information once you obtain it or have access to it. Having information is imperative, but knowing what to do with the information—or what it means—is vital to master the forces of sex, money, and power dynamics in relationships.

The knowledge and presence of sexual or financial information can have negative or positive results if used as a weapon in divorce, child custody, and business negotiations or dissolution. Revenge porn refers to sexually explicit content or video that is distributed without a person's knowledge or consent, to settle an imbalance of power.

Consider a scenario wherein an individual whose sexual images or content is under threat of exposure, makes a bold decision to pre-empt others' exposure and distribute their own sexual images. The result is still home-produced pornography, but the individual has chosen to expose the images of their own accord. The power of the information is in the controlling, or in this case distributing, of the information. Such was the case of Jeff Bezos and his 2019 "dick pic scandal," when the *National Enquirer* threatened extortion, lest they release his naked below-the-belt images. The bravado he displayed by deciding to expose his images himself, flipped the script on the *Enquirer*, thus controlling his own narrative and the information to be shared. In the decision to undermine their threat, he dissolved their control of him and the situation.

My mother's triumphant decision to empower herself and pay the bills promptly ended my father's incessant inquisition about her spending. He was no longer exposed to her shopping and spending forays, and her decision to pay the bills empowered her. The non-traditional role-reversal eased his anxiety about money, although my parents continued to squabble about other financial matters.

For years, my mother assailed my father's investment decisions, yet she never attempted to educate herself about what the financial statements meant, where he invested their savings, or how best to maximize their earnings. She preferred instead, to sit and quarterback from the sidelines about financial returns and investments.

When my father passed away, my mother was forced to learn all the things she chose to avoid. She was neither ignorant nor incapable of understanding these financial matters. She may have been afraid of feeling overwhelmed or befalling the same critical fate to which she assigned my father, but the irony was that at last she had to put her money where her mouth was. She either had to trust others to help her make sense of financial investments, or teach herself what the quarterly reports meant. Either way, she suddenly had choices, and she could no longer claim passive indifference or blame my father for his financial outcomes.

EMPOWERED

Knowledge is Power – an apt and exquisite proverb. While the origins and authorship of the aphorism are widely debated, its essence is understood: Knowledge is more powerful than physical strength. Knowledge is the most valuable thing in the world. Sex, money, and relationships can come and go but knowledge can never be taken away from us. Knowledge is power because we use it to think for ourselves. Knowledge gives us power to grow, love, and connect. Knowledge is where we begin our journey toward autonomy and independence; no one can prosper in life without it. Knowledge allows us to grasp the truth. Knowledge is our true power.

In the words of Søren Kierkegaard, "If I were to wish for anything, I should not wish for wealth and power, but for the passionate sense of the potential, for the eye which, ever young and ardent, sees the possible. Pleasure disappoints, possibility never. And what wine is so sparkling, what so fragrant, what so intoxicating, as possibility!"[6]

EPILOGUE

This book was completed during the most turbulent times the modern world has ever known. These words are not hyperbole. On March 11, 2020, the World Health Organization's Director-General declared the COVID-19 outbreak a pandemic. People everywhere began their version of shelter-in-place. The world changed overnight and entered into a new normal, a reality yet to be determined.

At the time of this writing, I am home, sheltered-in-place, treating clients, and running groups via telehealth. The extent to which our lives will be altered is still unknown, but our relationships have already been significantly impacted. Many families and relationships have experienced a death or illness of a loved one (in some cases more than one), stress related to the absence or presence of a partner under quarantine, heightened anxiety, and domestic violence. COVID-19 is having its way with us.

Global panic gave way to global protests when George Floyd—one more black American man—was murdered by police. George Floyd's death became a flash point fueled by decades of systemic racism, income and racial inequality; abuse of power. In the words of the American Psychological Association, "We are living in a racism pandemic."

The *Battle of the Titans* is not just a literary metaphor—it is a literal irony too great to ignore. I wrote that to fully understand relationships is to bear witness to historical events of its greatest paradox: power. When I began this book, my desire was for the reader to gain insights and skills to help shift an imbalance of power and control in their relationship. That is still my desire.

My hope now is that we harness the force of our empowered selves and work together in a shared battle against exploitation and abuse of power in all its forms. An adaptation of a previous passage is relevant: *The successful path through this historical choke point is our collective self-empowerment; the power that we derive from believing in our self—on par with caring about others and not forsaking self.* We can be our own obstacle or our greatest advocate.

Fear is paralyzing. Overcoming obstacles takes courage. When I was younger, it was clear that I had to grow out from under my father's enmeshment. Although that decision was frightening, it felt right, because my path forward involved undetermined outcomes; not good or bad, just outcomes that were yet to be realized. My decision meant rejecting the current known and accepting an uncertain outcome that I would need to live with.

Self-empowerment requires courage to take action even when the action is hard or frightening. In an uncertain world, one thing is not. Feeling powerless is not the same as abdicating our power.

ADDENDUM ON ATTACHMENT

John Bowlby's and Mary Ainsworth's efforts in the field of child development and attachment research paved the way for subsequent research delivering differential theories on the sequelae of attachment classifications. In Dr. Inge Bretheron's, *The Origins of Attachment Theory: John Bowlby and Mary Ainsworth*, Bretheron, a former student of Mary Ainsworth, distinguished professor, and noted researcher in internal working models of attachment relationships had this to say:

> More recently, interest (in) adult attachments has broadened to encompass marital relationships (Weiss, 1982, 1991) and has taken a further upsurge with work by Shaver and Hazan (1988), who translated Ainsworth's infant attachment patterns into adult patterns, pointing out that adults who describe themselves as secure, avoidant, or ambivalent with respect to romantic relationships report differing patterns of parent-child relationships in their families of origin.[1]

Several distinct paths of attachment research grew out of Bowlby and Ainsworth's seminal work. One such path, led by Dr. Mary Main, a former student of Mary Ainsworth, produced *The Adult Attachment Interview* (George, Kaplan, & Main, 1985, 1996), an interview procedure for assessing adults' narrative of self-identification, prevention, and protection from perceived dangers. In particular, these perceived dangers are tied to intimate relationships. In their research on adult attachment in relationship, Dr. Kim Bartholomew and Dr. Phillip Shaver emphasized interview measures with behavioral observations, work that grew out of Ainsworth's initial research on the subject.[2]

The second, independent path of research included the collective work of Dr. Cindy Hazan, Cornell University and Dr. Phillip Shaver, University of California, Davis, who were investigating adolescent and adult loneliness. Hazan and Shaver were personality/social psychologists, and according to Bartholomew and Shaver, "their work was quickly assimilated by other such psychologists, who tend to think in terms of personality traits and social interactions, be interested in normal subject populations, prefer simple questionnaire measures, study relatively large samples, and focus on adult social relationships, including friendships, dating relationships, and marriages (Bartholomew & Shaver, 1998)."

Bringing the two divergent paths together, Drs. Bartholomew and Horowitz proposed an expanded model of adult attachment (Figure 1.) that included **two forms of avoidance**. To assess this model, they used a self-report measure of experiences in close relationships in general (by revising Hazan and Shaver's measure) as well as two interviews: one focusing on childhood experiences (along the lines of the AAI) and the other focusing on peer relationships, including friendships and romantic relationships (Bartholomew & Horowitz, 1991).[3]

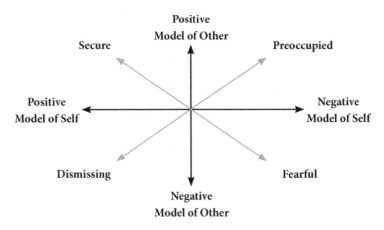

Figure 1. *Two-dimensional four-category model of adult attachment.*

Rudolph Schaffer and Peggy Emerson theorized that children could direct their attention to any available person. However, they noted that by the sixth or seventh month of life most normal infants selectively direct their attention to one person. "It is from this particular person that they seek proximity and from whom they object to being separated."[4] Thirty years later, in 1994, Drs., Hazan and Shaver, went on to hypothesize that our early displays of attachment are the same systems that govern our adult romantic relational interactions. What Hazan and Shaver specifically found in their work was a distribution of adult attachment categories. Those being, "55% secure, 25% avoidant, and 20% anxious/ ambivalent that has subsequently been replicated in many studies in several different countries (e.g. Feeney & Noller, 1990; Hazan & Shaver, 1987: Mikulincer, Florian, & Tolmacz, 1990)."

The list of preeminent researchers that include Bowlby and Ainsworth and continues today is extensive and would be too plentiful in numbers to include here. However, in 1987, a direction of research was continued by Drs. Hazan and Shaver. They hypothesized that adult romantic love is an attachment process similar to and consistent with the biosocial process formed in earlier life between infants and their caregivers. Their work centered on the research developed by Bowlby and Ainsworth, et al., regarding development of attachment bonds in infancy and were translated into terms appropriate to adult romantic love.

The work of Hazan and Shaver focused on Secure, Anxious, and Avoidant attachment styles, three patterns identified by Ainsworth, Blehar, Waters, & Wall (1978) in their studies of infant-caregiver attachment which is of particular importance when discussing attachment styles, emotional avoidance/ anxiety, and sex addiction. "A [later] study by Leedes (1999) regarding adult attachment styles among sexual addicts found that these individuals have a significantly higher rate (95%) of insecure attachment styles in adult relationships than the 44% found by Hazan and Shaver (1987). Since those with insecure relationship styles are more likely to have problematic relationships (Marchand, 2004), sexual addicts would be expected to be at greater risk for problematic adult romantic relationships due, at least in part, to their insecure attachment styles."[5]

Later in 1998 Drs. Brennan, Clark, and Shaver expanded on work previously conducted by Drs. Bartholomew and Horowitz (1991) with their publication of the *Experiences in Close Relationship Questionnaire* (ECR) indicating that, "individual differences in attachment can be measured along two roughly orthogonal dimensions: attachment-related anxiety and avoidance. A person's position on the anxiety dimension indicates the degree to which he or she worries that a partner will not be available and responsive in times of need. A person's position on the avoidance dimension indicates the extent to which he or she distrusts relationship partners' good will and strives to maintain behavioral independence and emotional distance from partners."[6]

Drs. Fraley, Waller, and Brennan (2000) expanded on Brennan, Clark, and Shaver's (1998) Experiences in Close Relationships (ECR) questionnaire with a revised update (ECR-R) (Figure 2). The two axes of anxiety and avoidance were expanded "to assess individual differences with respect to attachment-related anxiety (i.e., the extent to which people are insecure vs. secure about the extent of their partner's availability and responsiveness) and attachment-related avoidance (i.e., the extent to which people are uncomfortable being close to others vs. secure depending on others)."[7]

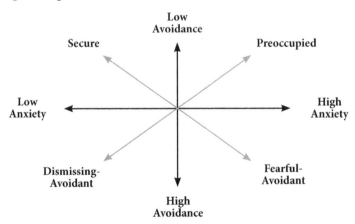

Figure 2. *The two-dimensional model of individual differences in adult attachment.*

To date, much work has been already been accomplished from the original work of Bowlby and Ainsworth but there is a need for more empirically-driven studies measuring adult romantic attachment. Consider the following summary in *Romantic Love Conceptualized as an Attachment Process,* by Drs. Hazan and Shaver (1986):

"Love and loneliness are emotional processes that serve biological functions. Attachment theory portrays them in that light and urges us to go beyond simpler and less theoretically integrative models involving concepts such as attitude (e.g., Rubin, 1973) and physiological arousal (Berscheid & Walster, 1974) For that reason the attachment approach seems worth pursuing even if future study reveals (as it almost certainly will) that adult romantic love requires additions to or alterations in attachment theory. It would not be surprising to find that adult love is more complex than infant-caretaker attachment, despite fundamental similarities."[8]

Hazan and Shaver continued to explore Bowlby's ideas but from the context of adult romantic relationships. They went on to say that the emotional bonds that develop between adult romantic partners arise to some degree from the same early attachment behavioral system about which Bowlby postulated. Both investigators went on to research and publish extensively on observed parallels between the infant-caregiver attachment behavioral system and the adult attachment behavioral system, and hypothesized that the latter may simply be an outcropping of the former. Adult romantic love, they argued, "is a property of the attachment behavioral system, as well as the motivational systems that give rise to caregiving and sexuality."[9]

Mikulincer and Shaver (2003, 2007) proposed that a person's location in the two-dimensional conceptual space defined by attachment anxiety and avoidance reflects both the person's sense of attachment security and the ways in which he or she deals with threats and distress. People who score low on these dimensions are generally secure and tend to employ constructive and effective affect-regulation strategies. Their ability to handle both the intra and inter psychic distress allows for emotional and relational flexibility, thereby ensuring a more successful outcome during times of stressful interaction.

On the other extreme are those who score high on both the attachment anxiety and the avoidant attachment dimension. These individuals suffer from attachment insecurities and tend to rely on what Cassidy and Kobak (1988) called **secondary attachment strategies**— deactivating or hyper-activating their attachment system in an effort to cope with threats. Deactivating strategies are employed by those who actively distance, deny attachment needs, and avoid closeness and interdependence in relationships. Those characteristics comprise the Fearful-Avoidant attachment spectrum. Due to attachment figures that disapprove of and punish closeness and expressions of need or vulnerability, these individuals register high anxiety and avoidance in relationships despite desiring to connect and wishing to bond.

Those scoring high on attachment anxiety and low on avoidance tend to rely on hyper-activating strategies—active attempts to achieve closeness and proximity, love and support. However, childhood experience established that attempts at connection will produce an inconsistent, at times hostile and angry, connection with significant caregivers. "These reactions occur in relationships in which an attachment figure is sometimes responsive but unreliably so, placing the needy person on a partial reinforcement schedule that rewards persistence in proximity-seeking attempts, because they sometimes succeed."[10]

Gurit E. Birnbaum, Israeli psychologist and researcher with the Interdisciplinary Center (IDC) in Herzliya, Israel, has focused her research interests on romantic relationships, human sexuality, and evolutionary psychology. Findings derived from Birnbaum's research with attachment dimensions and sexual and romantic relationships illustrate the need for additional understanding of how our attachment and sexual systems mutually influence each other at different stages of relationship development. Consider the following work by Birnbaum:

> More avoidant individuals, in contrast, feel uncomfortable with the closeness inherently involved in sexual interactions and, therefore, tend to detach sexuality from psychological intimacy (Mikulincer & Shaver, 2007; Shaver Mikulincer, 2006). This detached stance may account for diverse avoidance related sexual behaviors and motives, such as experiencing sexual fantasies in which they and the object of their fantasies are represented as interpersonally distant and alienated (Birnbaum,

2007b) engaging in less-frequent sexual activities with relationship partners (Brassard, Shaver, & Lussier 2007), reliance on the solitary sexual activity of masturbation, engaging in emotion-free sex (e.g., one-night stands; sex with casual partners), and having sex for relationship-irrelevant, self-enhancing reasons (see the reviews by Cooper et al., 2006; Mikulincer & Shaver, 2007). When more avoidant people do have sex with their romantic partners, they tend to experience relatively strong feelings of estrangement and alienation and display low levels of physical affection (Birnbaum & Reis, 2006; Birnbaum et al., 2006; Birnbaum, 2007a). Overall, more avoidant individuals seem to have a sex life relatively devoid of affectional bonding, even within the context of ongoing romantic relationships."[11]

The field of attachment and adult relationships vis-à-vis sexual and emotional behavioral systems is experiencing exciting developments due to joint technological and psychological advances. At the same time, cultural mores are shifting and redefining our individual "need" for relationship. In a world that has produced digital communication, virtual sex and relationships, and holographic incarnations, we are on the threshold of a newer realm and future meaning of attachment. With collective global research being forged on many fronts, it is clear that the field of attachment is experiencing a psychodynamic and dynamic paradigm shift.

NOTES

INTRODUCTION

POWER

1. Keltner, D. (2016, May 18). "Why Leaders Must Give Away Power in Order to Keep Influence," Fortune.

CHAPTER ONE

PUTTING POWER IN PERSPECTIVE

1. The concept of "good enough parenting" was introduced by Bruno Bettelheim, an Austrian-born author in his book, *A Good Enough Parent*, originally published in 1987. Bettelheim borrowed the concept of the "good enough mother" from Donald Woods (D.W.) Winnicott, a British psychoanalyst and pediatrician. Winnicott is influential in the field of object relations theory and developmental psychology; specifically, infant attachment.
2. Twohey, M, Kantor, J. (2020, February 7). "This Is the Toughest Question Facing Harvey Weinstein's Jury." The New York Times. Retrieved from https://www.nytimes.com.
3. Mead, N. L., Baumeister, R. F., Stuppy, A., & Vohs, K. D. (2018). "Power Increases the Socially Toxic Component of Narcissism Among Individuals With High Baseline Testosterone." Journal of Experimental Psychology: General, 147(4), 591–596. https://doi.org/10.1037/xge0000427
4. Study conducted by CNBC and LinkedIn between April 18-27, 2018.
5. "Survey: It's Still Tough to Be a Woman on Wall Street - but Men Don't Always Notice." (2018, June 26). Retrieved April 21, 2020, from https://www.cnbc.com/2018/06/25/surveyon-wall-street-workplace-biases-persist---but-men-dont-see-t.html
6. Ibid JBoorstin. "Survey: It's Still Tough to Be a Woman on Wall Street - but Men Don't Always Notice." CNBC, CNBC,

26 June 2018, www.cnbc.com/2018/06/25/surveyon-wall-street-workplace-biases-persist---but-men-dont-see-t.html."

7. McEnery, T. (2019a, January 14). "Thank God There Is No Sexual Abuse On Wall Street." Retrieved from https://dealbreaker.com/2017/11/thank-god-there-is-no-sexual-abuse-on-wall-street

8. According to research conducted and published by The Intercept, a nonprofit news organization, in partnership with The Investigative Fund, since 1998 only a handful of sexual harassment lawsuits have been brought by men. This information was accessed in a public database maintained by the Financial Industry Regulatory Authority (FINRA), which is Wall Street's self-governing organization, and overseen by the Securities and Exchange Commission. Among the 14 cases identified, four men won their arbitrations, one received an award on an unrelated claim, eight lost, and one resulted in an expungement. "Overall, the men fared better than the women, winning their harassment claims 29 percent of the time, compared to 18 percent for women." The Intercept 4/18/2018. https://theintercept.com/2018/04/18/in-30-years-only-17-women-won-sexual-harassment-claims-before-wall-streets-oversight-body/

9. Guinote, A., & Vescio, T. K. (2010). *The Social Psychology of Power* (1st ed.). New York City, NY: Guilford Publications.

CHAPTER THREE

OUR FAMILY – THE POWER OF HUMAN ATTACHMENT

1. Bowlby, J. (2005). A secure base: Clinical applications of attachment theory (Vol. 393). Taylor & Francis.
2. McLeod, S. (2009). Attachment theory. Simply psychology.
3. Fraley, R. C. (2016). Attachment through the life course.
4. Ainsworth, M., Retrieved from https://adoptioninchildtime.org/bondingbook/attachment
5. The Strange situation was a procedure devised by Mary Ainsworth in the 1970s with a sample of 100 middle-class American families. These observational experiments can be viewed on YouTube.

6.   The ECR-R is a 36-item self-report measure of attachment free to those who are interested in determining their own attachment style. The ECR-R is a self-report assessment, not a diagnostic tool; therefore the results are informational only and non-diagnostic in nature.

CHAPTER FIVE

Narcissism and the Winds of Shame

1.   O'Donohue, W., Fowler, K. A., & Lilienfeld, S. O. (Eds.). (2007). *Personality Disorders: Toward the DSM-V*. Sage Publications.
2.   Schulze, L., Dziobek, I., Vater, A., Heekeren, H. R., Bajbouj, M., Renneberg, B., ... & Roepke, S. (2013). Gray matter abnormalities in patients with narcissistic personality disorder. Journal of Psychiatric Research, 47(10), 1363-1369.
3.   The term was coined by Paulhus, Delroy L; Williams, Kevin M (December 2002). "The Dark Triad of personality: Narcissism, Machiavellianism, and Psychopathy". Journal of Research in Personality. 36 (6): 556–563. The triad is referred to as "dark" because of the malevolent qualities of the behaviors. Individuals who possess these traits tend toward exploitation, manipulation, criminal behavior, and sociopathic interactive styles of relating.
4.   W. Preston Lear, The Modern Icarus Complex: A psychoanalytic complex manifest in BASE jumpers and other action sports athletes, (ProQuest, UMI Dissertations Publishing, 2011), Accessed on December 5, 2012.

CHAPTER SIX

The Dark Side of Power

1.   Dr. Kevin Dutton teaches social psychology at the University of Cambridge and is a Research Fellow at the Faraday Institute of Science and Religion at St Edmund's College.
2.   Jones, D. N. (2014). Risk in the face of retribution: Psychopathic individuals persist in financial misbehavior

among the Dark Triad. Personality and individual Differences, 67, 109-113.

3. An interview with Esther Perel, psychotherapist on the paradoxical union of domesticity and sexual desire based on her 2007 book, Mating in Captivity. Accessed online at https://www.youtube.com/watch?v=wDw0STkffls

4. It is important to note that our sexual templates are forged in early childhood and adolescence. Sexual arousal can link to pain or anger that originates in traumatic experiences and is later re-enacted in adult life. Not all sexual arousal involving pain or anger is automatically deemed a trauma reenactment. Professionals who specialize in trauma and addiction must attend to the phenomenology of an individual's sexual experience before assigning a pathological lens. Healthy sexual expression such as BDSM, or kink play can be intense and involve elements of power and control dynamics within an intense yet safe dynamic. BDSM (Bondage/Discipline, Dominance/Submission, and Sadism/Masochism) is the umbrella term under which kink falls. BDSM can contain some, all, or none of the sexual behaviors that involve humiliation, revenge, or retaliation.

5. Weiss, R. (2020, February 3). Eroticized Rage. Retrieved from https://www.psychologytoday.com/us/blog/love-and-sex-in-the-digital-age/202002/Eroticized-Rage.

6. The term "revenge porn" refers to the nonconsensual uploading of sexually explicit material to humiliate and intimidate the victim. As of 2019, there are no federal revenge porn laws. There are 41 states and the District of Columbia with laws that define revenge porn, to varying levels of prohibited behavior and penalties as: any person, with the intent to harass or annoy another and who publishes or distributes electronic or printed material or video content showing the victim's genitals, anus, or female breast of the other person, or depicts that person engaged in a sexual act. In the majority of cases the victims are overwhelmingly female and the abuse is perpetrated by a former male partner or lover.

7. Several years before I wrote *For Love and Money*, Patrick Carnes invited me to train the staff of a noted treatment

center. A section of the training involved the concept, Eroticized Rage. Later that day, we both noted that sex fused with anger (Eroticized Rage) and money fused with anger are driven by the same underlying issues. Thus, we mutually refer to this dynamic as Monetized Rage.

8. Jeanfreau, M., Noguchi, K., Mong, M. D., & Stadthagen, H. (2018). Financial Infidelity in Couple Relationships. Journal of Financial Therapy, 9 (1) 2. https://doi.org/10.4148/1944-9771.1159

CHAPTER SEVEN

Leveling the Playing Field

1. Lammers, J., Stoker, J. I., Rink, F., & Galinsky, A. D. (2016). To Have Control Over Or To Be Free From Others? The Desire For Power Reflects A Need For Autonomy. Personality and Social Psychology Bulletin, 42(4), 498-512.

2. William Ury, *The Power of a Positive No*, (New York, Bantam, 2007), 107.

3. Barrett, L. F. (2017). *How Emotions Are Made: The Secret Life of the Brain.* Houghton Mifflin Harcourt.

4. Chris Voss, interview with Dax Shepard and Monica Padman, Armchair Expert with Dax Shepard, podcast audio, February 6, 2020, https://armchairexpertpod.com/pods/chris-voss

5. Fearless Girl, Commissioned by State Street Global Advisors, March 7, 2017, New York.

6. Søren Kierkegaard, Either/Or: A Fragment of Life (1843)

ADDENDUM ON ATTACHMENT

1. Inge Bretherton, "The Origins of Attachment Theory: John Bowlby and Mary Ainsworth," Developmental Psychology 28 (1992), 759-775. (http://www.psychology.sunysb.edu/attachment/online/inge_origins. pdf).

2. Bartholomew, K., & Shaver, P. R. (1998). Methods of assessing adult attachment: Do they converge? In J. A. Simpson & W. S. Rholes (Eds.), *Attachment Theory and Close Relationships* (p. 25–45). Guilford Press.

3. K. Bartholomew, L.M. Horowitz, "Attachment styles among young adults: A test of a four category model." Journal of Personality and Social Psychology 61 (1991): 226-244.

4. H.R. Schaffer, P.E. Emerson, "The development of social attachments in infancy," Monographs of the Society for Research in Child Development, (1994).

5. J.L. Zapf, J. Greiner, J. Carroll, "Attachment Styles and Male Sex Addiction," Sexual Addiction & Compulsivity 15 (2008): 158–175.

6. M. Mikulincer, P.R. Shaver, "An attachment perspective on psychopathology," World Psychiatry. 11:1 (2012), 11–15, Accessed: July 29, 2012.

7. T. Ein-Dor, M. Mikulincer, G. Doron, P.R. Shaver, "The attachment paradox: How can so many of us (the insecure ones) have no adaptive advantages?," Perspectives on Psychological Science, 5 (2010), 123.

8. C. Hazan, P.R. Shaver, "Romantic love conceptualized as an attachment process," Journal of Personality and Social Psychology, 52:3 (1987), 511-524.

9. Ibid.

10. J. Cassidy, R.R. Kobak, as quoted in M. Mikulincer, P.R. Shaver, "An attachment perspective on psychopathology," World Psychiatry. 11:1 (2012), 11–15, Accessed: July 29, 2012.

11. Gurit E. Birnbaum, "Bound to interact: The divergent goals and complex interplay of attachment and sex within romantic relationships," Journal of Social and Personal Relationships, 27, (2010): 245-252, Accessed November 2, 2012.

INDEX

Index

ABOUT THE AUTHOR

DEBRA KAPLAN, MA, MBA, LPC, CSAT-S, is a licensed therapist, author, and speaker. After a successful career on Wall Street, where issues regarding sex, money, and power are legendary, Ms. Kaplan merged her fascination with narcissism and control with her studies in psychology. Her first book, *For Love and Money: Exploring Sexual & Financial Betrayal in Relationships,* is the inspiration for her trainings and intensives geared to those who wish to understand the hidden dynamics of sex, money and power in relationship. Debra is an invited guest on podcasts and radio programs. You can learn more at:

www.debrakaplancounseling.com

THE ACCOMPANYING WORKBOOK
TO *BATTLE OF THE TITANS*
ANTICIPATED PUBLICATION DATE 2021

Made in the USA
Monee, IL
23 June 2021